Erase the Problem of Bullying

Jill Ammon Vanderwood

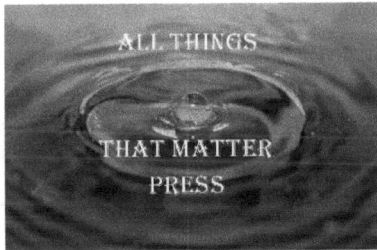

ALL THINGS
THAT MATTER
PRESS

ISBN: 978-996663403

Library of Congress Control Number: 2015948559

Cover design by All Things That Matter Press

Published in 2015 by All Things That Matter Press

Table of Contents

Section Four: Bullying Because of Race

Section Five: Bullied Because of a Disability

Section Six: Bullied Because of Religion

Section Seven: Learn from the Experts

Introduction

Ever since I was a young girl, I've heard the Bible story of Joseph. Joseph was the favorite son, and his father gave him a coat of many colors. Because they were jealous of their father's favoritism, Joseph was bullied by his brothers. He was pushed into a pit and left to die, and then the brothers changed their minds and sold him into Egypt. They took his coat and dipped it in lamb's blood, telling their father that he had been killed.

Then there was the story of Goliath, who taunted the people and wanted someone to come fight him. Finally David came with a sling and challenged him. The giant who tormented the people was killed with one stone.

Over and over in fairy tales, we read about a bully who scares innocent people or animals. Those who were bullied include the Three Little Pigs, Little Red Riding Hood, Hansel and Gretel, Snow White, Sleeping Beauty, and many others. Those who are powerful in some way, whether they are bigger, have larger teeth, or have a group egging them on, set out to make life miserable for others. This has been going on since biblical times and still exists in schools, churches, playgrounds, neighborhoods, and even in families. No one has the right to treat another person unkindly because they are different.

Sometimes we call this bullying, and sometimes it's harassment or discrimination for sexual orientation, the color of their skin, or physical or intellectual handicaps. Whatever it is, it's wrong.

What Would You Tell Kids Who are Being Bullied?
by James Donaldson

James Donaldson is an NBA All-Star

***

The things I would tell kids who are being bullied:

- Make sure that it's actual bullying that's taking place and not just good-natured teasing (sometimes it's in poor taste) which all kids go through.
- If it's painful (physically, mentally, or emotionally) it's probably bullying, especially if it goes on for a period of time.
- If it's not painful (physically, mentally, or emotionally), it's likely that you're being teased, and you're embarrassed by that. None of us like to be teased, but that happens from time to time and you have to realize that's what it is.
- I feel that the best way to overcome it is to work hard and become good at something. Find something you are really good at, and then become even better. If you play music, become a better musician. If you're an artist, become a better artist. If you play sports, be the best player and teammate you can be. If you get good grades in school, strive to be the very best you can be and keep your aim and your goals high. Find friends who enjoy the same things you enjoy. Don't lower your standards to match the bully's.
- Try not to get into a confrontation with the bully. If he/she is calling you names and trying to provoke you into a fight, don't fall for it. Usually it's when the bully sees that they are "getting to you," or "getting under your skin," that they've done what they wanted to do to you in the first place. Try to keep your composure and don't let them see you get rattled.
- Realize that often bullies are immature, unsure of themselves, don't have many friends, and are trying to prove that they are tough guys/girls. It's lonely being the bully.

Section One

How Bullying
Affected My Life

"Secrets Are Weapons That Can Be Used Against You"
~Jill Ammon Vanderwood

Sharing a Secret
by Abby

Abby was thirteen when she wrote this.

***

I had a secret about my mom being a stripper. The word got out because my sisters told their friends and they told other people. Boys at school who didn't even know me would say, "Can I meet your mom?" and ask if my mom would give them a lap dance. I said, "No," and it would just get worse and worse. It's just not fair for people to judge me for what my mom does. The kids would say I'm the whore and slut of the school, just because my mom's a stripper.

A Parent Was the Bully

Hi, I'm Abby, I'm thirteen years old, and I live In Utah. I have been bullied and decided to share my story along with others who have been bullied. It all started around the second grade. I had a lot of friends at school, and two friends in my neighborhood. I would play with them every day after school. But one day I went over to a friend's house and her mom told me I wasn't allowed to play with her daughter anymore, even though she had met my mom and allowed her daughter to sleep over and come to my birthday party. My other friend wouldn't play with me, either, because she wanted to play with the other girl. All at once I had to walk to school alone and play by myself, even though I saw my friends playing together.

At first I had no idea why she couldn't be my friend anymore, but in the summer before I went into the third grade, I was walking past her house with my sister Amber, who knew about my problem. Amber told me she was friends with my friend's sister. Amber had been honest with her and said, "My mom is a stripper." I then realized that her mother was holding this against me, and that made me very upset. I didn't want my mom to be a stripper. I was a little girl and I had done nothing wrong.

Supporting Our Family

My mom was a single mother trying to support three kids without child support from any of our fathers. My dad injured his back in a four-wheeler accident and had surgery when I was around two years old.

My mom tried working as a cocktail waitress at first, but when she realized the dancers were making much better tips, she tried out for a job as a stripper. She made good money and we were able to live in a better house and dress nicer than we did when we lived in the 'ghetto' apartments where we use to live.

Most people who work as strippers are trying to make a better life for their families, pay for their education, or pay off debt. My mother always says that it's not breaking the law—it's a legal profession. Most of the time, moms don't make as much money as dads and can't pay the bills without child support. My mom worked because of her family.

More Problems

The next year, after being bullied by my friend's parents, I moved houses and changed schools. In fourth grade, I met a girl named Annika. We were best friends until the middle of sixth grade. For a year and a half, we had been like peanut butter and jelly—we stuck together. In fifth grade, I had made another friend named Nikki, who was new at our school. Nikki, Annika, and I were great friends. Then the word got out once again that my mom was a stripper. This all happened because my other sister, Kelly, had told *her* friends that our mom was a stripper, and her friends are big brothers and sisters to my friends. This time the problem got much worse. Kids in my class started calling me hurtful things like slut, whore, and hoe.

Nikki and Annika didn't call me names during this time, but they didn't stand by me, either.

When nearly the whole class turned on me, I was unhappy every day. I couldn't get away from the teasing and name-calling, and I absolutely *hated* it! All at once I didn't have anyone to sit with at lunch or anyone to hang out with at recess.

When I really needed a friend, a girl named Jamie would always be there. She stayed with me whenever the class was rude to me. We were really close and we never got in fights.

Asking for Help

One day when my grandma came to read to my class, I was crying in the hall and didn't want to go to class. She asked me what was wrong. When I told her the bad things the kids in my class were calling me, she talked to my teacher. My teacher said that I brought it on myself because I was boy crazy. My grandma said, "No, it's not Abby's fault." Then my grandma asked if I could talk to the principal. My teacher let me go to the office.

The principal pretty much told me to suck it up and just get through it because she couldn't make anyone like me. She couldn't force them to be nice to me and I understood that, but what could I do if no one would help me? I didn't feel any better after talking to the principal. I thought she could help the kids to show respect for me and ask them to stop glaring at me and calling me names. The principal didn't handle it very well.

Up In Smoke

I would often fake being sick just so I wouldn't have to hear those nasty words. In the sixth grade, things got better. Once again I had Nikki and Annika as friends, along with my new friend, Jamie. I was so happy with my best friends. We had a lot of fun.

But one day after lunch, I went into the girls' bathroom with all my friends. I heard Nikki say, "Oh, shit, I forgot my lighter." I looked over and she had a bag of weed. Someone told the teacher that Nikki had weed and that I was smoking it with her.

We both went to the office and I was like, "No, no, no! I was just in there and then I walked out."

Nikki got suspended for trying to smoke weed in the girls' bathroom. When she came back to school, she bragged about it. Most of the girls she hung out with thought she was cool, but I didn't want anything to do with it. We stopped being friends. She thought I was the one who told on her, but it wasn't me.

There was a new girl named Monroe in school. She and Nikki are now like sisters. Annika also decided to leave me for Monroe. I liked my other friends, but I cried for days when Annika left. I missed her. We had been friends since the fourth grade. Annika just left with Nikki and Monroe after all we had been through together. I should have remembered that when the whole class turned on me in the fifth grade, Nikki and Annika weren't my true friends. I realized later that I wasn't really able to be myself around them because I tried to be like them by wearing makeup and dressing a certain way.

Monroe was being really rude and trying to fight Annika. Even after Annika left me, I was there for her and tried to defend her. She was so upset that she literally cried on my shoulder, and then a week later she started to ignore me again and hang out with Monroe. I was like, "Well, I guess that was your last chance."

Annika never gave me a reason for leaving me, so I have given up on being friends with her now and I don't even talk to her.

Finding True Friends

Once again, the name-calling began with "Eew. What a whore." And "Why would anyone like her?" I hated that, but Jamie stuck with me and introduced me to Shannon and Isabella. Now I am best friends with all three girls. I don't really mind the stuff the other kids say about me because I realized that as long as I know it's not true, then it doesn't really matter. And as long as my friends stay with me, then I shouldn't really care about what someone else has to say.

The old group of friends doesn't treat me well and when they talk about me, they talk in Spanish, so I don't know what they're saying. I'm not Mexican so I don't understand a word of it. One of my friends who can speak Spanish tries to translate for me. It's not fair for Nikki to be saying stuff about me in Spanish so I can't defend myself. That would be like me speaking Italian and saying, "You're a whore" while the other girls laugh and she can't say anything about it.

I don't know if Nikki has been in trouble with drugs since then because I don't get in her business.

A Spy for Nikki

There was a girl named Emily who pretended to be our friend. I hung out with her and we went skating together. It wasn't until Nikki and Monroe threatened to beat me up that I realized Emily had been a spy for Nikki. We were all called into the principal's office separately. Emily admitted to being a spy. This created a big drama circle and it was all Emily's fault.

Another time, I found out from Monroe that she had been talking to one of my new friends, Shannon, on Facebook and saying all these dirty things about me, and telling her that they were going to beat me up. We all went to the principal's office—Nikki, Jamie, Shannon, Emily, Monroe, and I—but all at separate times. No one got in trouble, but the principal pretty much said that I didn't have proof they were going to beat me up, so I was making a big deal out of nothing. I said, "My safety is sort of important, and if I don't feel safe at this school, then what's the point of going here?"

I had seen what Monroe said from Shannon's Facebook page: "Why are you friends with Abby? She's fake and she's a whore. She has nothing good to do with her life."

First they took away my friend Annika, and then they tried to turn my new friend Shannon against me and threatened to beat me up. Now I don't even talk to the mean girls. I also make sure I don't talk about them to anyone, after Emily told them everything I said about them.

***

"When another person makes you suffer, it is because he suffers deeply within himself, and his suffering is spilling over. He does not need punishment; he needs help. That's the message he is sending."

~Thich Nhat Hahn

"Someone who used to like you can find more reasons to hate you."

~Jill Ammon Vanderwood

When Friendships Change
by Riley

Riley wrote this when she was twelve.

***

Have you ever been bullied?

I was bullied in the fifth and sixth grade by kids in my class.

I'm a girl, but when I was in the fifth grade, there were three boys I used to play with on the playground. Two of the boys got mad at Andrew and didn't want to hang out with him anymore. I still liked Andrew and still talked to him. When the other two boys saw me talking to him, they started hitting and kicking me on the playground, and this continued even in the classroom.

I felt sad because we all used to be friends. I saw them bully and tease others as well. If anyone had a fat body figure, they bothered them all the time and told them how fat they were.

I saw them bully a third grader while they were in the fifth grade. She was practicing throwing and catching footballs so she could get better, and they told her she couldn't play anymore. They also started following her after school and tried to pop her football.

How did the bullying start? Did you tell anyone?

The other boys made this little crew with boys from the class, along with their younger brothers. They wanted to put me on their crew of people who were no longer friends with Andrew. I didn't know that they added me. One of the boys just started beating me, saying, "You can't just leave the crew."

In the sixth grade, one of the kids stopped hitting me, but the other kid continued to hit and threaten me, saying if I told the teacher, he'd make up something bad about me. I told my teacher in secret. After I told on him, he stopped hitting me when the teacher was around, but he hit me whenever my teacher wasn't looking. I tried to make him laugh so he wouldn't be so mean, but when he said he was going to tell a really funny joke, the joke involved hitting, so he hit me.

Has he ever really hurt you?

Yeah, one time he kicked me in my knee. It felt like it popped out of place and I couldn't walk. The teacher knew about it because he did it right in front of her. After that she kept an eye on him in class, so if he went near my desk, she told him to sit down. If he didn't sit down immediately, he got a Stop and Go, which meant he was in trouble.

Every recess, I hung around three girls. One of my friends was really tall, and whenever the bully came around, we walked away, trying to avoid him.

Did you talk to your parents or a family member about the problems you are having with this boy?

Yes, I talked to my older brother. My brother's junior high was right up the street, so after school, if I hung out with Andrew, my brother would pretend like he was just walking around with his friend Justin. But he'd actually watch to make sure I didn't have any problems.

Did that help?

Yeah, things got much better because the bully wouldn't bother me in front of my teenage brother.

I didn't want to tell my parents or my grandma because I didn't want them to go to the teacher or embarrass me in front of the class. My grandmother worked in my classroom a couple days a week, and she knew the kids. I was afraid that if I told her about the bullying, she might have said or done something that would make things worse. Or maybe my grandma wouldn't believe me, because she likes the kids and they never bully me in front of her.

Sometimes when a boy hits you, he really has a crush on you.

Yeah, the one who kept hitting me did have a crush on me. His dad died when he was in the fifth grade, and he took his sadness out on other people because he didn't have a dad and he was jealous of kids who have their families.

Oh, so you kind of understand him?

Yes.

If I was hanging out with Andrew and the other boy came up and we ignored him, he would get really mad. One of us would say, "Have patience, calm down." But instead of calming down, he would throw a basketball at us. Rather than giving him attention for that, we would just walk away, and that made him even madder.

So he has an anger problem, and it's probably caused by his dad being gone.

My grandma always says that if someone is being a bully, that means they are being bullied themselves. If someone is mean, something is probably happening to them at home. I could understand that he was having problems at home, but that didn't give him the right to be mean to others. I always thought that I didn't cause his problems so he had no reason to be a bully to me and Andrew. If he continued to be a bully, before long he wouldn't have any friends left.

***

"Making a thousand friends is not a miracle. A miracle is making one friend who will stand by your side when thousands are against you."

— Marianna Miller

Two Stories About Bullying:
Ashley's Story
by Ashley, and
A Story About Katie as told by Ashley

Ashley wrote her stories at the age of fifteen.

***

My name is Ashley, and I am now fifteen and in the tenth grade.

In the second grade, I had a bully named Bradly, but everyone called him Brad for short. I have always been tall for my age, and Brad only came up to my eyes. I never knew why Brad bullied me. First it started with name-calling, and then progressed to him telling people secrets that he overheard between my friends and me. One of these secrets was about a crush my friend Karen had on a boy. When kids in class started whispering and telling Karen's secret, she was mad because I was the only one she had told her secret to. One day during recess, someone told me that Karen was going to kill me. I didn't believe them because she was my friend.

While playing on the field, I stopped for a breath. Karen came up and put her arm around my neck and her other hand over my mouth while tackling me from behind. In order to get away, I had to elbow her in the chest to knock the wind out of her. She ran to the playground monitor on duty to get me in trouble. I was the one who got in trouble and was given detention. But once they saw the marks on my neck, she got suspended from school. I must say that was the worst year of my life, because not only was I being bullied at school, but I lost a good friend because of Brad and his big mouth. I also lost another friend that year who died of cancer. He was only eight years old.

When I was in the third grade, I was still being picked on. I had recently gotten glasses, and the same bully encouraged other kids to call me "Four Eyes." I was also called "Giant" because I was so tall. I hated myself for being tall. During the summer, I had hit a parked car while riding my bike and broken my nose. Even though it healed quickly, somehow Brad found out. After that, he told me I was so ugly that my nose broke itself.

That year he wasn't only mean, but he began to physically abuse me. One time he tried to hit me in the face with his head, and he broke my new glasses. I was too afraid to tell my mom how they broke, so I told her I dropped my glasses, and she was so mad at me. We have a large family and we really couldn't afford new glasses.

The bullying didn't stop until I started taking the rude things Brad was saying and turned them into compliments. When he called me Four Eyes, I would say, "At least four eyes are better than two." After he saw that I would no longer put up with his rudeness, the bullying stopped.

I didn't see Brad for a couple years until one day in the summer when I spotted him at a water park. He didn't really recognize me until I told him, "I'm Ashley." I saw that the look on his face was one of sorrow for what he'd done to me.

There is no way Brad or anyone like him would try to bully me now. I've always been taller than him, but now he barely comes up to my shoulder. I am still trying to forgive him for the two years of my life that I didn't really get to enjoy being a kid.

***

"Love can quickly turn on you. Hate can turn to love, and love can turn to hate."

~Jill Ammon Vanderwood

***

There were two girls who bullied Katie throughout junior high. The problem was even worse because Emma and Angela were her best friends up until the time they turned on her. Angela started to call her ugly, and would say "eew" whenever she walked home from school. Katie's home was just past Angela's house, so Katie had to walk by her on the way home. Sometimes Emma went home with Angela, so she helped her call names. Other times, Emma would threaten to beat Katie up. Katie was scared of Emma, but not Angela. The name-calling definitely got worse whenever Emma was around.

I became friends with Katie in the second year of junior high, and in the third year, we were like sisters. Since I started walking home with Katie, the bullies were afraid to hurt her or call her names. They could no longer call her "a friendless loser" because they could see that she no longer needed their friendship and no longer cared what they said or did. Every once in a while, they still called Katie names or called her ugly, but I told her to keep walking and not to pay any attention to them. After I got to know Katie better, I suggested that she could turn things around by taking the insults as compliments, and that is what she started doing. After that, when they called Katie ugly, she would tell them, "Thank you for the compliment," and walk away.

Since Katie and I are "sisters," some people even ask if we're twins and we tell them "yes." Katie even dyed her hair the color of mine, so we would look more alike. She hasn't seen Emma or Angela since the last day of school. Katie and I are having such a good time with our friendship that she doesn't even care about the other girls anymore.

***

"Rather than joining in the taunting of others, include them in your circle of friends. By doing so, you will create lasting friendships."
~Jill Ammon Vanderwood

Smelling like Garbage
by Jason

I was bullied in the sixth grade by a boy who started out being my friend. When I got into junior high, I witnessed most of the seventh graders being bullied by the ninth graders. I think the older kids must have also been bullied when they were in seventh grade and passed it on, more like a tradition or initiation. In high school, I became a bully without realizing it.

What was your bullying experience?

When I was in the sixth grade, there was a new kid in my class and I was the first one to become his friend. He told me about his home life, and it seemed pretty bad. He was raised by a single mom who was a drug addict. His dad was in prison and they were really poor. He was only twelve years old and he told me he had been in trouble with the law quite a bit. I'm pretty sure it was for fighting and for stealing.

After he came to school, he spent the first two weeks trying to make friends and trying to fit in. I don't know what caused the change in him, but he started picking on everyone. He didn't just pick on me, but he turned on everyone at that point.

I would have continued to be his friend, but when he started bullying, it not only changed my attitude toward him, but he lost any chance of having a friend.

He didn't just call names. It was physical bullying. He would push people down and try to start a fight. This new kid was real mean physically to all the other kids. He would randomly come up behind a classmate, trip him, and walk away. I felt sorry for him, since I had been his friend and knew about his problems at home, but I never fed in to his behavior. I could see that the kids who yelled back or pushed back just made it worse, but he seemed to lighten up after one kid beat him up.

Did you fight back?

At first I didn't want to fight back because he was the new kid, and I thought that if I got in a fight with him, I would get blamed and I would be in trouble.

Toward the end of the year I started pushing back, but not until after another kid, who had enough, fought with him. By then, all the boys in the class who had been afraid of him decided we were through with this bully as well.

Was that the only time you were bullied?

When I was in the seventh grade, there were a group of ninth-grade boys who would pick on all the new seventh graders. One at a time, four ninth graders would throw one seventh grader into a garbage can. It was just kind of a hazing thing.

Even though I was never thrown into a garbage can, I noticed a lot of other seventh graders coming out smelling like garbage.

Do you know why you weren't bullied?

I honestly think I escaped the bullying because they had a crush on my older sister, Kim. If guys in the ninth grade picked on me, they knew they wouldn't have a chance of going out with my sister.

So did you defend your friends?

No, but I did help them out of the garbage can.

Did the bullies get caught?

I don't think so. It's possible that they had been bullied as seventh graders, so they turned around and bullied seventh graders once they were older.

Were you ever a bully?

For the most part I got along with everyone, but in seventh grade, my friends and I would pick on this really big girl in one of our classes. Her name was Nichole, and we used to call her Nicow. I don't know why we did that. As I grew older, I realized that it made her feel bad about herself, and I felt horrible.

Fifteen years later, she found me on Facebook. I'm so glad I got a chance to apologize to her for all the mean things I said and did to her back in junior high and tell her how terrible I felt about it. She accepted my apology. That was four years ago and we have been friends ever since.

My advice to others is that it is way better to be nice to everyone around you because then you have much less chance of being bullied. You are also less likely to end up doing or saying something you will regret later. Chances are, the person you are picking on and bullying in the fourth grade might be someone you would want for a friend in the ninth grade, and they won't like you because you bullied them. Or you might want to be friends with a boy you like, but that person won't want anything to do with you because someone told him you used to be a bully. Be nice to everyone, because you want them to treat you that way.

***

"I hate knowing that my life will be harder just because I'm not pretty."

~Sairra@Zayls Awsome

My Frizzy Hair
by Rachel Doherty

Rachel is from the United Kingdom.

***

I think most individuals suffer some form of bullying in their lives. For me it started pretty early, around age seven or eight; an age when children begin to understand group culture and target those who don't fit in. I was a bit of a teacher's pet, a keen reader, and eager to do well at school, traits that can often result in name-calling. I also carried a little extra weight when I was younger, "puppy fat" which I would attribute to my parents' divorce. The incidents in primary school were challenging at the time. I would often be upset at the mean words of other children and did not enjoy going to school just to be their victim, although sooner or later they'd get bored and someone else would be in the spotlight.

The more serious bullying occurred in secondary school, where the name-calling became much more graphic and difficult to deal with. I wore glasses and had bangs with curly, frizzy hair, didn't wear makeup, and was prone to bad skin. My physical appearance was usually the first thing I would be teased about. I wasn't the only one to be targeted. A group of "popular" girls had formed, and anyone who didn't do what they did was instantly deemed "not cool." Verbal abuse would often follow. In an attempt to stand up for others, I made the situation worse for myself.

These popular girls drank on weekends and would brag about it, they were cheeky to teachers, and generally caused mischief wherever they went. Any time a member of staff became involved, the girls who caused problems would group together and get their story straight. This often left me looking like the troublemaker rather than the one suffering from the problem. At the lowest point, the girls used intimidation and physical abuse by circling me in the hallway at school and not allowing me to pass by them, or pulling my hair whenever they saw me. My attendance began to slip rapidly. Their words and actions affected my self-opinion, my happiness, and my studies.

One girl in particular kept drawing on my arm with red paint in the middle of an art class while calling my mum names. I gripped her hand and told her to stop. That resulted in us having a physical tussle. We had each other by the arms and were attempting to hit each other, but the teacher didn't even notice. The same girl threatened to "get" me after school at the bus stop. After school, she called me names and pounced on me with an audience watching. This time I fought back. Somehow, I got her into a headlock and told her never to pick on me again because she wasn't as tough as she thought she was. If she did bother me, she knew now that I would fight back. She never attacked or belittled me again.

I don't condone violence, and the physical fight I was involved in was the result of one and a half years of constant verbal abuse. In the end, I felt backed into a corner and had to do something for them to leave me alone. The teachers must have recognized by this stage that the gang of friends was problematic. They divided them into different classes, which diluted their power and influence.

Eventually, with time, the issue of bullying, experienced by many within my school, began to disappear. I made a commitment to myself never to allow anyone to abuse me or make me feel so low again.

As often happens in cases like this, you could say I have had the last laugh. When I got older, I began using hair-straightening irons to smooth my frizzy hair. I got contacts, and my skin cleared up, so the things they picked on me for didn't exist anymore. Although I was once considered ugly, I would now say I am far from it.

I am doing well in my chosen career. I am about to graduate from University with a degree in Public Relations, Marketing, and Advertising. I work with companies to help them increase their profits by assessing their marketing activity and helping them to improve on areas such as their website, writing style, brand identity, and integrating social media into their communications.

I think the bullying I suffered has made me the person I am today. Now I am much more strong-willed and determined to succeed. Being the target of bullying was in no way a pleasant experience and was one that, at the time, I am sure I would rather not have gone through.

It's unlikely you will make it through life without coming across someone who is in some way mean, unfair, or rude to you. If you're prepared by knowing how to deal with bullying, you are likely to learn from the situation, and the experience may actually be beneficial to you in the long run.

Social networks, such as Facebook, have allowed me to see how those who bullied me are getting on in life. Many of them are either unemployed or unqualified for good jobs, and some have been teen mothers.

Bullying comes in many forms and will feel different to each person experiencing it. Don't give up or feel helpless; confide in a family member, a teacher, or a friend. Remember, it won't last forever—your time at school is brief and, in the end, those who are bullied are often the people who end up in the better situations as adults.

***

"If everything you say gets laughed at…
then you become afraid of everyone…
and are no longer able to speak…
Your heart…
….shuts down…
And your words die…."

~Natsuki Takaya, *Fruits Basket, Vol. 5*

Erase the Problem of Bullying
by Jill Ammon Vanderwood

You can help to erase the problem of bullying by speaking up for those who can't speak up for themselves. Being bullied in school turned me into an introvert. I would never speak up in class or in a group. This led me toward my career as a writer. I always had a lot to say and found writing as a way to express myself.

I was the new girl in the fifth grade. Most of the kids in my class had known each other since kindergarten. I moved from the country to a city. Everything was different, including the level of learning, and the games we played at recess and P.E. I was shy and kind of lost in my new school, but I did make a few friends.

When I dropped my eraser, a boy named John picked it up and wouldn't give it back. I knew my mother wouldn't buy me a new one if it was lost, so I told the teacher. The teacher told him to give it back to me. After I told on John, I overheard some of the other boys in the class planning to "get her back."

This small event triggered several years of bullying. All the boys in the class gave me trouble all day, every day for the rest of the year. They called me names, shoved me, and threw nasty notes on my desk. When someone would bump me, they would say, "Eew! I got Ammon germs." Someone even started calling me an Ammonite, which was an undesirable race of people from the Bible.

One day, my reading group was putting on a play where a boy had to put a shoe on my foot. All the other boys commiserated with him for having to touch me. The next day, that boy went home during lunch recess to get a gas mask for another boy who had to sit next to me in class.

Things were so bad with the boys in the class that the girls decided to vote for me as class president. There were more girls in class than there were boys, so they actually pulled it off. This action caused more booing and jeering than ever. I got up in front of the class and couldn't call anything to order. After a few minutes of the ridicule, I said, "I resign," and sat down. They then began to cheer because the candidate that all the boys voted for was put in as president.

I had a talent of playing the harmonica and tried out for the talent show. I thought I could prove I was good at something, but they wouldn't even let me play without jeering.

The next year, I didn't have as many problems because there were only a few of these boys in my class. I only had trouble with them when I saw them in the hallway or outside the school. A couple of the boys were cousins, and they carried on with the abuse long after the others left me alone. They also had younger brothers who began bullying my younger sister in her class. She really resented me for the treatment she was getting because of me.

When my sister and I would walk home or play on the playground after school, we had to be on alert for these two cousins and their younger brothers. They called us names and spit in our hair, or chased us while riding around on their bikes. Have you ever had someone spit in your hair? First, you can smell their bad breath, and then the spit drips. I had to walk home from school with the disgusting smell, holding my long hair out so it wouldn't drip on me. During the summer, one of the boys threw eggs at us while we walked home from our summer job of picking berries. We constantly had to be on the lookout for these pests and often changed our route or got off at another bus stop and walked a mile out of our way.

The nonsense all but stopped until I got into the seventh grade. I made friends with a new girl. I confided to her that I had a crush on Ricardo, a boy who lived near me; she told him I liked him. When other kids found out, the jeering and taunting began again. He started it all up, even though he hadn't even known me in the fifth grade. A boy named Paul who worked with me on a history paper in the eighth grade confided to me that anyone who was friends with Ricardo "has to hate you." This continued up until high school. Once I was in a new school where I could get lost in the crowd, I could finally be myself and get away from the bullying.

In high school, I became an introvert. I never raised my hand and I never spoke up, even when I had something to say. I didn't want to do anything that would call attention to me. I usually walked to school alone, but one day a guy came up to me and said, "Hi, do you mind if I walk with you?"

"No," I said. But my mind reeled. I had things to say to him, but I walked with him and never said a word. This was the boy who'd brought the gas mask to school in the fifth grade.

When I was in the eleventh grade, I had a new boyfriend. While we were in a music store together, Enrique, the brother of my short seventh-grade crush, happened to see us. My boyfriend knew him and said hi. Enrique took my date aside and told him not to get involved with me. My boyfriend later told me, "Enrique doesn't like you, but I do." That seemed to be the end of it.

One lost eraser, and the bullying continued until the eleventh grade.

***

This year, I started connecting with old high school friends. Someone recommended that I add the guy who spit in my hair as a Facebook friend. I looked him up and saw pictures of his family, then ignored it. The recommendation kept coming, so I wrote him a note, saying, "It's kind of ironic that Greg wants us to be friends when we were far from ever being friends."

He wrote back and said, "Hi, I remember you. How are you doing? I guess we weren't friends because I was very shy in high school."

My sister confronted this guy's cousin at a class reunion. He is now a school counselor who deals with problems like bullying. He said he doesn't remember me and doesn't remember treating me badly. It's interesting that neither of them had any sleepless nights over the way they treated me. I, on the other hand, had a hard time going to school day after day. I couldn't even get away from the bullying after school or in the summer.

I have always made sure to include people who are being left out, and I have always had a large group of friends around me. I carried the self-esteem problems created by bullying for much of my life. It was years before I could open my mouth and speak in front of people, not wanting to call much attention to myself.

I really think that being an introvert has helped me develop my talents. I learned to write down my thoughts and feelings, and that led to a career as a writer. My writing also led to public speaking. Now I speak to groups of kids at school assemblies, scout troops, and church groups. I also teach workshops to other writers.

Section Two

Stories From Bullies

"Pay attention to your enemies, for they are the first to discover your mistakes."

~Michelle Dinsda

My Life as a Bully
by Jacki

Jacki is from Wisconsin.

***

Why do people bully? That is an important question that can probably be answered in many different ways.

I will answer the question for myself. I remember starting to bully kids while I was in elementary school. There's not one particular incident that stands out in my memory as the reason I started my bullying behavior. However, I do have some theories.

My mother and father got divorced when I was six. My younger brother and I went to live with my dad, and my half-sister stayed with my mom. I really didn't see them much after that. My mom was irresponsible and didn't follow through with many of her visitations.

After a few years, my dad got into a relationship with a single woman with no kids, and eventually married her. This caused some backlash with my mother, who was asked to pay child support. Rather than pay child support for children she couldn't commit to or afford, my mother agreed to relinquish all parental rights so that my stepmom could adopt us.

I was about eight years old when we, as a new family of four, moved to a new home and I changed schools. With all the changes in my life, I felt shy about meeting new kids, but I was able to make the adjustment.

My dad worked in a factory doing welding, grinding, and other manual work. Shortly after the wedding, I noticed that my dad was drinking. Apparently he already had this problem, but he was able to hide it while dating my new stepmom. She was well educated as a teacher, and has never been a drinker. I think the new school and the tension at home might have contributed to me acting out as a bully.

I don't recall seeing myself as a bully, but I was one of the class clowns who liked to make people laugh. My parents were both raised on farms, and things like fashion, makeup, decorating the house, and socializing were not important to my new mother.

Therefore, having any trendy clothes was not in the cards for me. I was often embarrassed about what I had to wear, compared to the other girls. I was also embarrassed to have friends come home with me, as our house did not compare to many of my classmates' homes.

Then there was my father. It was apparent that this "drinking thing" was a big deal to my adopted mom.

Things at home were not cheery, with lots of arguments, crying, and blaming going on. Besides, we were not a family who showed physical affection, and I really don't remember a whole lot of "I love you" being said.

The bullying came in because I didn't want to be teased. If I could continue to make people laugh or focus on the problems of others, I thought I was doing a good job of covering up. In an alcoholic family, there are certain roles that family members take on—mine was the scapegoat. I recall hearing my mother saying things like, "If you would just get better grades, or didn't get in trouble at school, then maybe your father wouldn't need to drink." They certainly couldn't fight about a perfect daughter with perfect behavior, now, could they? My brother was the baby, and therefore he was coddled and protected.

At school, there was one girl in particular I would mimic or harass. She got very upset, but my classmates thought it was funny. This continued for most of elementary school. When people laughed at what I was doing, I felt as though they were accepting me. I also remember picking on a very shy girl. Every time I said something mean, she would just giggle. Giggle? I tried harder to get a reaction, but still nothing but giggles. I respected her for that, and from then on, I left her alone.

I have always been small, and now that I'm full grown, I'm all of five foot one and a half inches and a hundred and five pounds. I have never been a physically threatening person. I have always been an athlete, so maybe people thought I was tough. I sure could talk the talk. I would only stick with my close friends and did not trust people or myself enough to branch out and make new friends. I would try to float between groups such as the dirts, meaning kids who smoked and might drink some or experiment with drugs. They were also the troublemakers. Then I'd hang out with the athletes for a while before switching to the alternatives, who were into music and different dressing styles. I never felt like I fit in. I enjoyed the power of intimidation, and no one called me out on it. What a rush. Did I ever feel bad? Occasionally, but my own life was so messed up, I would take whatever attention I could get.

By the time I got into high school, my dad had been in and out of rehab several times. Once he tried to sober up on his own, which landed him in the hospital due to extreme symptoms of withdrawal. Another time, he almost killed himself from driving drunk. He passed out with a .3 alcohol level and crashed his truck.

I ran away from home when I was sixteen because I wanted to see my biological mother and half-sister. I moved in with them, and my adopted mom and dad had an attorney sign guardianship over to my mom temporarily so she would have to be responsible for my actions. I found out why I was kept from her: she would take me to bars to drink on school nights so we could spend time together. She couldn't be bothered to change plans. I watched her get bombed and bring home different men. She asked me to drive without a license because she was drunk, but I had also been drinking.

I returned to my father's house and graduated from high school three months pregnant, with a lot of soul searching to do.

When my parents found out I was pregnant, they kicked me out of the house, forcing me to live with my boyfriend and his parents. I went through a controlling, abusive relationship with my boyfriend. When my son was born, I decided I needed to be a better person for him. I finally found the confidence to leave my baby's father. I then met a wonderful guy, and I also let God into my life. I married the new guy and we learned to live our lives to be pleasing to God. Along with that came many ongoing changes and transformations.

Today, when I come across people who knew me from school, they can't believe I'm the same person.

My dad had now been sober for eight years after trying a new rehab program. He had changed his life dramatically and we give God the glory for this. Dad is on his final semester of finishing his two-year accounting degree. Our relationship today is awesome, and I am very blessed to have such a caring loving father. He is very happy now and he's a wonderful grandfather.

My adoptive mom and I were on the outs for a while, but after my son was born we got closer. She was a great help with the baby. We have both changed and now we have become the best of friends.

I also keep in touch with my birth mother. Even though I love her and forgive her, I don't overly expose myself or my children to her. We avoid getting involved in her problems, and I can't allow any of us to be emotionally hurt by her.

My boys are now fifteen and eleven, and my husband and I will soon celebrate being married fourteen years. I try to keep myself physically fit, and my husband and I sell real estate as a team in the central Wisconsin area.

***

"Trust can only go so far; make sure you have a backup plan."
~Jill Ammon Vanderwood

Jail is Full of Bullies
by Cedric Dean

Cedric Dean is an author and youth activist who has written a self-help book for teens and parents on bullying, among other topics. What is also unique about him is that he is a federal prisoner. Mr. Dean founded SAVE—Safeguard Atone Validate Educate programs—in 2009. One year later, in 2010, he received the Federal Bureau of Prisons' highest award, the Call to Service Award, becoming the first United States penitentiary lee inmate to receive such an honor. He is known throughout the prison as "a leader's leader."

Mr. Dean initiated the Save A Child Month Campaign in January 2012 to ask the nation to reach out to at-risk youth and those who undertake in adverse behavior such as bullying.

While in prison for life plus five years, Dean has helped hundreds of prisoners obtain their general education diploma and thousands more change their lives for the better. His books include For the Love of the Streets and How to Save Our Children from Crime, Drugs, and Violence

***

I was a bully. At age thirteen, I was introduced to a bully who taught me how to manipulate others to get what I wanted. I learned how to play on the fears of others. I was selfish and egocentric, and I only thought about getting my needs and desires fulfilled. Other bullies in my neighborhood told me that people who were richer than me owed me something. They would say, "The man owes us this, and the poor must take from the rich." I grew a hatred for white people and rich people. My mind was twisted to the point that I was a certified gangster.

Life Before Crime

I was born in Charlotte, North Carolina, growing up as the only child of a Christian single mother. My mom took me to church and taught me right from wrong. My mother forced me to be a Cub Scout and a choir boy, which ultimately made me grow resentment for church. I have always been a good student. I had a passion for learning as a child and teenager. And my passion only grew stronger as I grew older.

The lessons I started learning later were more devious and dangerous. I wanted a father figure, so I turned to the streets for what was missing at home. The streets taught me how to be a bully. The thug life provided me with a false sense of love and security. I felt a sense of self-dignity and self-pride. But the things that made me proud—bullying, robbing, manipulating, and intimidating—were things that caused shame to my family and former friends. Things changed because the adults around me weren't interested in the things that interested me. I loved to play sports, but the only people I had to play sports with were bullies, gangsters, and drug dealers.

I was reborn into a new world of crime, drugs, and violence. When I was sixteen, I was charged and convicted of robbery with a dangerous weapon and went to prison until I was twenty-one. Eleven months after my release in February, 1994, I was charged in a six-count federal indictment for conspiracy to distribute crack cocaine and possession of a firearm by a convicted felon. I was convicted of the charges on May 20, 1996, and sentenced to life plus five years.

My Mother

My mother has never given up on me. She has been the source of my strength from the beginning. When times got really bad, she prayed for me, encouraged me, and loved me unconditionally. I owe my very existence to Betty Dean Baker; her patience and persistence made me the man I am today. Her love has helped me see beyond these prison walls and reach out to kids who are heading to a life of bullying and crime.

Does bullying lead to crime?

All gangsters started out being bullies. I have been around the world's most notorious gangsters, in some of America's most dangerous state and federal penitentiaries, and every gang leader I've spoken to started out bullying around their neighborhoods and schools. One form of bullying leads to another. Every time a bully gets away with it, it emboldens him to take it to another level. It starts with taking a kid's lunch money, then his new shoes. It ends when you take his life because the kid decides to resist. In the '80s, I was incarcerated with teens who were sentenced to life for killing a kid over a starter jacket or a gold chain. I did five and a half years for bullying some kids out of a gold chain, so I know for a fact that bullying leads to crime.

Career

Seven years into my second prison term, I was placed in a special housing unit where I was confined in a cell for twenty-three hours a day. With a lot of free time on my hands, I read an urban novel titled "B-More-Careful" by Shannon Holmes, who had also served time in prison. I enjoyed the book so much that I started writing a book of my own, *For the Love of the Streets*. Mine is the tale of someone whose faith in God, willingness to change, strength, and infatuation to overcome barriers, impediments, and unusual odds can be a blueprint for anyone on the path of death and self-destruction.

My next book, *How to Save Our Children From Crime, Drugs and Violence*, is a self-help book which I published in 2010.

Serving a life sentence without parole, I had very little to look forward to when I wrote my first book in 2002. To fill my time, I enrolled in an inmate-taught creative writing class. Then I began reading books on writing and studied the styles of other writers, so I could teach others how to write. I was not expected to become a teacher and transform gangsters into gentlemen inside prisons, but I made a promise to the people who helped me along the way that I would help others who are living like I used to live. I didn't think it was possible for someone with a past like mine to be given the opportunity to teach anyone anything.

***

"Dean has himself crossed over the threshold of crime and violence to become the advocate for responsive change in our youth. I have proudly watched him mentor, teach, and apply tough love to redirect the pain, fears, and uncertainty of young prisoners into courage, dedication, and commitment. Cedric has done what many people have tried to do with our youth, but you must walk the walk and talk the talk." (Eugene Linwood, founder of Reaching Out Beyond Bars)

"His ability to focus his energy in a positive way has set an excellent example for many of the younger inmates who look to him as a leader." (Lance Cole, a Federal Bureau of Prisons Supervisor of Education)

***

How should bullying be handled?

People who bully other people are attention seekers. They are motivated by a lack of respect and recognition from others. One of the main tendencies of a bully is to get attention by any means necessary. So you have to give him the recognition he wants and needs in a good way. If you don't, he'll do whatever it takes to get it in a bad way. Bullies are very clever and convincing with their manipulation tactics. The only way to beat a bully is to be a tougher bully. Police officers and school officials must instill a sense of fear in them. There must be a zero-tolerance policy.

Bullies don't like consequences or resistance. When a person resists, they'll just find another victim who will be nonresistant. The only way to deal with bullying is by threatening bullies with dire consequences and educating them about the impact of their actions. We must make it easier for students to make anonymous reports of bullying at school. Likewise, have hotlines within the community to report it. It takes a community to stop bullying.

About SAVE

From prison, I started an organization called SAVE. Safeguard Atone Validate Educate is fully committed to addressing bullying. We have designed and implemented a New Life Curriculum Series that deals exclusively with specific aspects of bullying, i.e., learning how to communicate with bullies, identifying errors in behavior that cause bullying, understanding how to outsmart bullies, and other preventative measures. SAVE has transformed thousands of bullies into productive members of society. We have Leaders Breed Leaders seminars that allow bullies to see themselves as the world sees them. Character education is the crux of our program. We teach life skills classes, leadership classes, parenting classes, employability classes, and other self-awareness classes. We do public service announcements and we collaborate with law enforcement, school and public officials, and community organizations on prevention and intervention initiatives. January, 2012 was our Save A Child Month initiative. We received an overwhelming amount of support from citizens nationwide. We are doing everything we can to save our children and teens from premature death and incarceration. Every five hours, a child or teen commits suicide. We are committed to ending that trend.

In 2011, I collaborated with the Federal Bureau of Prisons and launched a replica of the SAVE program called RISE (Rehabilitate Integrate Stimulate Educate). The hearts, souls, and minds of each of you can rise. Power is not in violence. Power comes from your ability to use your mind. The more you think, the more powerful you become. I have dedicated my life to stopping the influx of teens and young adults entering prison for senseless acts such as bullying. Children need to know the consequences of their actions and decisions and the effect those actions can have on their lives, their family, and the people in their community.

***

"I applaud you, even while serving time in prison, for stepping up and taking responsibility for helping find a solution." (Kevin Jennings, the Assistant Deputy U.S. Secretary of Education)

***

What I would tell bullies?
Jail and hell are full of bullies. Neither is where you want to be. God don't like ugly. Bullying got me life plus five years in federal prison. Bullying has sent many of my friends to the graveyard. You can be a bully or you can be a leader. A leader is not a bully, and a bully is not a leader. A leader leads by example in a positive way. What goes around comes around. What you do to others will come back on you. Somehow … someway … someday.

***

In 2009, Dean's life sentence was reduced to four hundred and twenty months as a result of his exemplary work in stemming prison violence and changes in federal sentencing guidelines for crack cocaine offenders. He is currently working with his attorney to be released under the 2011 Retroactive Crack Guideline Amendment.

Cedric Dean is currently serving time in FCI Butner Medium II in Butner, North Carolina. He is still teaching GED and Adult Continuing Education classes for the Federal Bureau of Prisons and is currently enrolled in a business finance class.

***

"Hands are not for hurting but should always be used to better our world.

Always remember a bully never wins unless you believe their hurtful words and then it will keep you from truly living!"

~Timothy Pina

Making a Career of Helping
Others Fight Bullying
by Frank DiLallo

I am the author of Peace2U: Three-Phase Bullying Solution and Peace Be With You: Christ-Centered Bullying Solution, curricula for teachers and counselors. The manuals and workbooks are published by ACE Press at the University of Notre Dame. http://ace.nd.edu/press/ The model evolved from my bullying prevention work with public and parochial schools and is based on my own story of being a bully.

Check out my website at:

www.peace2usolutions.com<http://www.peace2usolutions.com

What made you decide to write about bullying?

It's been both confessional and personal. On a professional level, when I came to the diocese as a school consultant, there were eighty schools across nineteen counties in northwest Ohio, and fourteen of them were high schools. I started getting calls from principals about bullying. With my background as a licensed counselor, I tried the best I could and brought in experts for the areas where I felt weak or didn't have the knowledge or the background. I also went to trainings and workshops outside the diocese to learn more about bullying. Although I gained good information, I never felt like I walked away with solutions to the problem. I needed solutions that would be practical for educators and meaningful for students. So I thought, "Maybe I need to do something more with this."

I was getting calls from our principals to make classroom presentations. The more presentations I did, the more the idea or model evolved. Most of my assemblies and classroom presentations were for grades four through eight.

On a personal level, one of the things I noticed was that the more and more I responded to bullying problems in the schools, the more I was taking an introspective look at how I had behaved when I was in school. And one of the things that became very apparent to me was that I bullied classmates while I was growing up. I started to feel a lot of shame and remorse as these memories came to the surface. As I worked on the problem of bullying on a professional level, it began to evoke emotion in me about the damage I had done. Part of this process—call it my penance, if you will—was to create a positive ripple instead of the negative ripple that I created growing up. So my work to help students who have bullied, been bullied, or were witnesses of bullying has been a very powerful transformation and inspiration for me in my professional world and for me internally. It's my own psychology of taking a look at myself.

I can't imagine what you must have gone through when you realized that you were a bully.

Yeah. It's startling in a way, but also liberating to own it and take responsibility for it. When I talk to teachers, I tell them never to take bullies at face value, that there's something underneath it. There's a trail to it, and we need to ask the right questions, like who treated you like that?

My father was a drill sergeant in the Army during the Korean War. He had an angry edge, and when things weren't just right, I became a whipping post.

Sometimes we'd play a game where he would hit me in the arm. This really wasn't a game, and it was very hurtful to me. If I didn't flinch or cry, I would get a chance to hit my father in the arm. Of course I never won. I was put into a position in my own home where I felt helpless and I didn't have any power over my environment. My acting out at school was caused by identifying with my own aggressor, my father. I took the behavior he modeled for me and did the same thing to fellow students. I became a victim-turned-offender. I believe that 99.99 percent of the time, bullies have some history of either being bullied at school or being abused at home. There's something that can be traced back to the bully's past. If somebody wakes up one morning and says, "I'm going to take this out on another human being," there's some underlying circumstance.

How did you take it out on other students?

When I was a fourth grader, I went around the playground hitting students in the arm. Somebody must have told on me because the teacher asked me to come over to her. She looked me in the eye and said, "Frankie, did you hit Joey?"

I said, "Yeah," and I said it with entitlement, like he deserved it. She didn't say anything to teach or redirect the behavior. It was a cold day and she was carrying leather gloves. She wadded them up and swatted me across the face. That didn't leave a very lasting impression on me because her reaction didn't make me want to change my behavior. It was interesting how her disciplinary action backfired. It caused me to justify that I would continue with my current behavior, and it even strengthened my sense of entitlement. This behavior continued into the seventh grade.

What became apparent to me is that bullying isn't only between two people. There's always a third party involved, and it could be one person or multiple third parties or witnesses. Here is a poem that I wrote about being a seventh-grade bully:

The Code of Silence
It was an ordinary day not much different from all the rest,
Eric, Tommy, and Frankie in 7th grade taking a different kind of test.
Tommy is tall, thin, and picked on by most of the class.
Eric is short, stout, lots of hot air and a voice full of brass.
Frankie is tall, strong, with less brain and more brawn,
Always trying to prove he's better than, by making everyone his pawn.
The three boys find themselves in the restroom at Guy Middle School.
Eric standing in the corner playing it so calm, so cool
With his arms folded and leaning back against the cold block wall.
Frankie and Tommy were standing in front of an unfriendly bathroom stall.
Suddenly the tension mounts and Eric shouts in a loud sarcastic tone,
"We should hit Tommy and do whatever we can to make him moan!"
Eric shouted even louder, "We don't like Tommy, we don't like his kind!"
The tension was high and like a puppet possessed, Frankie lost his mind.
He began to hit Tommy in the upper right arm; he hit him with all his might.
Tommy stood stiff trying not to flinch even an inch, not wanting to show any fright.
Eric got louder and louder. "Hit him harder!" he yelled, while counting every blow.
Just like a movie director, this active bystander was surely running the show.
"We don't like odd numbers," as he counted along with hit number five.
"We don't like even numbers," taunting and provoking to keep this insanity alive.
Tommy didn't do anything. He never fought back, he never even muttered a word.
Why is it he didn't do something to stand up for himself, how

strange, how absurd.

Somehow, someway, this frightful bullying triangle came to a screeching halt.

Three boys in a restroom, just an ordinary day, who would you say is at fault?

Three boys casually walking out of this nightmare and back to class just shows

The code of silence, not telling, is so very strong, because no one else knows,

The bully, the bystander, and the target will forever keep this shadowy secret and shame.

All three boys will never forget the damage done; they will always feel the pain.

Many, many years have gone by and you would think this would all just go away,

But every decision we make and how we treat another is always here to stay.

Every hurtful action, every hurtful word, leaves a lasting imprint on others.

Why not treat everyone with respect, dignity, like equal sisters and brothers?

Just like an etching in granite, what kind of impression do you want to make?

We only have but one life to live, so treat yourself and others well, for God's sake!

Everyone deserves our very best, no matter what their beliefs or color of their face.

Treat others with kindness, love, and support, because we are all one in this human race.

~Frank A. DiLallo
November 2005

There are two kinds of bystanders: active and passive. Eric was a very active bystander because he was screaming out, "We don't like Tommy. We don't like his kind." His energy came across as chaotic, hectic, and it was very contagious. So, like a puppet possessed, I began hitting Tommy in the arm, but Tommy didn't do anything. He didn't say stop, didn't walk away—he didn't do anything. That was really remarkable to me.

I would be considered the bully because I went along with what Eric prompted. I think we need to look at the bullying behavior that is encouraged by the active bystander. Looking back at my own situation, it became clear to me that bullying is bigger than just a few individuals.

There's actually a social contagion that gets created.

So now you're making a difference, and it's making up for what you did.

Hopefully. I want to take what I've done and turn it around and make it useful for students to look at their own lives and their own behavior and ask themselves the question, "What kind of contribution am I making to the classroom? What kind of contribution am I making to this school? What kind of legacy am I leaving?" As a result, I make a ripple effect. It not only extends from the classroom into the school, into the community, and into the state, but into the country and into the world. I want the students to realize that everything they say and everything they do has an impact, whether positive or negative. I also want them to take an honest look at the impact they are making and have the opportunity to shift that impact, if they don't like the legacy they are currently making. I wish to God that someone had given me those choices and had presented it that way for me so I could look at my behavior and make a shift. I also wish I could have communicated the helplessness I was feeling in my own family.

My father is in his eighties now, and the good news is that we have an incredible relationship because we improved our honest communication. He has read the books I've written about bullying and I think he's feeling remorse about it. My father has a different life now, and he's very proud of me and the work I've done. When we get together, we hug, we kiss, and we hold hands. I just love it! I know in my heart that I'm at peace, and we are at peace with each other, and it's glorious.

I tried to contact those whom I have bullied, but I can't find them. I have Googled them, but I come up short.

I hope to get schools in every state to pick up my books, which the schools in the diocese here are using widely. I have spoken in Houston and New Orleans, and that's not usual for me. When I went to Houston, it was so cool because most schools get fifty to sixty parents out to hear me speak, but the school in Houston did a lot of marketing and gave incentives to get the parents out that night. When I went into the auditorium, they had four hundred-plus chairs out. I was thinking, *"Come on,"* because I've never had that kind of turnout. At quarter to the hour, only half those seats were filled. When I was ready to start, every seat in that auditorium was full. It was incredible to have a parent audience of that size. I even had the chance to share a little bit about my story, too.

Section Three

Being Bullied for Sexual Orientation

"Everyone deserves our very best, no matter what their beliefs or color of their face. Treat others with kindness, love, and support, because we are all one in this human race."

~Frank A. DiLallo

Author's note: If you are being bullied because of race, gender, religion, disability, or sexual orientation or you think you may have a case of sexual harassment, your civil rights may have been violated. If this is causing you difficulty in learning because of fear, or other obstacles such as not being able to try out for a team, being left out of activities, name-calling, et cetera, this is more than bullying and now falls into the category of harassment. If you have reported the harassment and nothing has been done to correct the problem, you may have a case against the school as well as the students causing the harassment. Ask for a copy of the school's harassment/civil rights policies, or go to the school district. If you have evidence of the harassment in the form of video, audio, or pictures of marks left on you physically, this will be very helpful for your case. (Information from William Preble, The Center of School Climate in Learning and the American Psychological Association American Civil Liberties Union Model Anti-Harassment and Discrimination Policies for Schools)

Writing My Story
by Zack Van Den Berge

Zack Van Den Berge is the author of Inanimate Heroes, *about a boy who was bullied because he was gay.*

***

When I was a kid, I was always different. I loved making people laugh, and so I would do silly things even as a small child for laughs. The first time I heard the word "fag" was when I was skipping down a hall and it made the older kids laugh. I thought they were laughing because I was being silly, not at me specifically. When I was in about sixth grade, I began to realize that it wasn't me just being funny anymore. It seemed as soon as I realized that, the bullying got much worse. I was called "queer" and "fag" on the bus the entire ride home, and I would often sit in the front seat crying while the kids in the back shouted. But then, in seventh and eighth grades, I was fine. I made a bunch of friends and was pretty much friends with everybody.

When I entered freshman year however, the bulling started all over again. In my book, *Inanimate Heroes*, the main character, Andy, tries so hard to go unnoticed. This was the exact same attitude I had. I thought that if I kept low and quiet, no one would notice me and I wouldn't have a problem. But I caught attention virtually the first day. My hair was, and still is, long and curly, so older kids would say I had "fag hair." What still haunts me the most is that I would try to appease these bullies. I straightened my hair, and one night I even considered cutting it when everyone in my house was asleep.

Then a boy from grade school recognized me, and, from then on, my freshman year was total hell. At first, it just started out with harassment on the bus. But it soon became daily bouts of torment and public embarrassment. I would have things thrown at me during lunch, be shoved while walking down the hallways, and have snowballs flung at me while waiting for the school bus. At one point, I was even hit in the back of the head with a half-empty bottle of soda.

But somehow I survived. I made it through my freshman year, and, just like grade school, made a ton of new friends. By the end of sophomore year, I had an entire group of people who were my friends; by senior year, I had more friends than I could count. I even won two class superlatives that my senior class voted on. Toward the end of my senior year, I was one hundred percent sure of what I had been ninety percent sure of my entire teenage life—I wanted to be a writer, primarily a novelist, but I just loved writing anything: poetry, essays, and even free articles. During my senior year of high school, I was searching for a meaningful subject for my first novel, something I could really anchor myself with and be passionate and proud of. One night, sitting with my laptop, the news popped on. It was in late September, I believe, and I heard on the news that thirteen-year-old Asher Brown shot himself.

My first thought was, "My God. That's such a shame. Another kid shot himself while playing with his dad's gun."

And then, as the story progressed, I found out that he purposely shot himself. It simply didn't register with my brain. Why would a thirteen-year-old boy feel he didn't want to live anymore? But as I read the bottom of the screen, the title of the news story further said "due to bullying." It might sound odd, but to me, it was like hearing about September 11th. I remember everything so acutely. It was one of those moments that you felt so quickly, but you didn't know what you were feeling right away, like cold water poured on you while you were asleep. At that moment, I knew what my first story had to be. I needed to tell my own story about being bullied.

Inanimate Heroes is a book about Andy, a gay freshman who lives in a small town and is going to high school. As the book progresses, he's found out by the primary bully, Jason, and has to endure multiple events of embarrassment and harassment, much like I did.

It also goes on to mention the various support structures that I used as a kid, which was actually where I derived the name for the novel. During that painful time in my life, I would read, write, and listen to music; I did just about anything to get my mind off what was happening. There were people who helped me, even though I never met them. Maya Angelou, Judith Sheindlin—Judge Judy—Amanda Palmer, and David Bowie indirectly gave me words of wisdom and comfort which helped me in some way, even though they were complete strangers.

I also have a great deal of respect for the YouTube "It Gets Better" project. They are giving kids a platform to speak their minds and telling them, "You know what? It's not going to last. You will outgrow this." I thought that was fantastic. It was absolutely the truth. We just need to get these kids to hold on to this truth. The only issue with sending this message to teens is that many probably don't buy into the message of "it gets better."

"Okay, it gets better, but what about now?" Teens are oriented in the present, and I'm sure that if anyone reading this looks in retrospect, they will realize that to be true. Nothing was more important than getting that note from Bobby Fisher or nothing was more important than passing Mr. Bruton's algebra class.

What I wanted to do for kids with *Inanimate Heroes* was to show them the middle ground. "It does get better, I can promise that, but here is what might happen until it does." I truly felt that people telling their own stories along with the message of "it gets better" was the best way to get young adults to listen.

Now, I won't lie to you. The adulation I received from being an author at nineteen was really a great feeling. I felt that I was truly taking a big step in the right direction for my career choice. But what made the biggest impression on me was a fifteen-year-old boy from Missouri. He was feeling sad and down, and he mentioned on a Facebook support group for gay youth that he needed someone to talk to. I commented something along the lines of "Message me whenever." I got a message telling me his horror stories from school that were so much like the story of my life when I was his age. I gave him the promo code for the free download of my book, which I usually only give to reviewers and critics, and said, "I wrote a book for just this sort of thing. Please read it." He seemed a little leery at first, but he downloaded *Inanimate Heroes* to his grandma's computer and started reading it.

Each day, he would report to me that he read a chapter and that the same thing he was reading had happened to him. He even said that someday he wanted to be a writer. At some point, he said, "Thanks so much for giving this book to me. It's helped me a lot." That short little thank you meant more to me than any compliment or accolade I could ever receive.

What I want to tell kids who are being bullied is simple, but I think it gets the point across. It does get better. I'm living proof of that. The prettiest, most vibrant of flowers often come from the filthiest of soils. Look at where so many of the people in this book, *Erase the Problem of Bullying*, have come from. You will make it through this, and you will be a much better person in the end. Also, if you've learned anything at all from reading this book, it's that you're not alone. I know all about the loneliness; I felt so isolated from everyone. When I think about it now, though, I would be hard pressed to find any person on this planet who has never endured some form of bullying. But we must go on. We must live to fight another day and help others. You are so special to so many people—maybe even people you aren't aware of, like Asher Brown was to me. You can't give up. Ever.

I also have a message to the kids who aren't being bullied, to the kids who sit adjacent to the bully or those who are bullied. Speak out. Say something about it. Bullies often get a lot of their momentum by thinking they are being funny or cool. Some don't honestly realize the real damage they are doing to the person who's subjected to their remarks. Make a simple statement. "Knock it off, you're not funny." If you're afraid the bully will turn on you, maybe you could say something to a teacher at the end of class. The worst you can do is nothing. I know it might be frightening to get involved, but bullies are, in my opinion, generally enormous cowards. Once they find out that they aren't in the majority, they will often back down.

Is this always the case? No. In fact, many people stood up for me, but it didn't deter my bully. At least you can say that you did *something*. If you're afraid to confront the bully yourself, maybe you can befriend the kid who's being bullied. That might be the best thing you could ever do for them. But I can't say it enough: please don't just let it happen and do nothing. In many cases, that's why it happens in the first place.

***

"Some people won't be happy until they've pushed you to the ground. What you have to do is have the courage to stand your ground and not give them the time of day. Hold on to your power and never give it away."

~Donna Schoenrock

Boys Will Be Boys?
by Patrick Dati

Patrick Dati is a survivor of childhood bullying, and, as a nine-year-old, managed to escape from a brutal attack by an unknown assailant. Mr. Dati now seeks opportunities to speak out against childhood traumas of all kinds, especially bullying, and in 2012 he was selected by the U.S Department of Health and Human Services as one of seven people who will be their spokesmen for their anti-childhood trauma efforts.

***

My brother is three years older than me, and he was the worst bully in my life while I was growing up. He bullied me for fifteen years and he still bullies me as an adult. My family knows that my brother abused me, but they have always covered that up.

When I was five years old and he was eight, he split my head open. My parents took me to the doctor to get stitches. When I was seven, he split my lip open, and my parents had to take me to the hospital to get stitches. Every time they took me to the ER, the doctor would ask, "What happened to your son?" Their excuse would be, "Well, you know, boys will be boys."

I kept all the problems from my childhood to myself, but my first wife knew something was wrong and had me see a psychiatrist. I was diagnosed with OCD, Obsessive Compulsive Disorder. I saw the psychiatrist for several years. He wanted me to write a diary. This process started three years ago, and I am now starting to speak publicly about bullying and I've been working on my book, which is now available through Amazon.com. The title is *I Am Me: Survivor of Child Abuse and Bullying Speaks Out*.

My book covers different aspects of my life, but the main focus is on the abuse and bullying from my brother. I also tell about being a gay man, which I hid for many years for fear that my devout Catholic family would turn against me. After I divorced my second wife, I knew that I was gay, and I could no longer pretend to be something else.

When I started to do research for the book, I found that eighty to eighty-five percent of men and boys never come forward about their abuse out of shame and fear, and I was alarmed to find that I was among those statistics.

My father died a couple years ago in October, and, the following

February, my family gathered at my mom's house for dinner. My older brother called me a faggot in front of my family and told me he had hated me for my entire life, and if I didn't leave my mom's house, right then and there, he would kill me. I turned to look at my family for support, but they all put their heads down. The last thing I said to them was, "You people are sick, and he's demented. He's a drug addict and an alcoholic, and none of you want to face him."

My brother called me a faggot again before picking up a knife and chasing me out of my mama's house. After that low point, I made the decision to break the cycle of discrimination and bullying by going public with my story.

I was nine years old when I was raped in the men's room at a department store. I was shopping with my brother and my cousins when I needed to use the restroom. I left my brother and cousin and went alone into the men's room. When I got into the restroom stall, I heard someone go out, and I thought they were leaving. I came out of the stall and washed my hands. When I turned to get a paper towel, I was startled to see a man standing near the door. I approached the door to leave, and he put his hand over my face. He put a knife to my neck and said, "You need to follow me to my car, and if you don't, I'll kill you." At that point, I started kicking and screaming. He tried to force me out the restroom door, but I think he knew he couldn't get me out to his car without people noticing. He then stripped me of my clothes and raped me, right there in the men's room. When he was finished, he put the knife to my neck again and said, "If you say a word, I'll track you down and kill you."

At the age of nine, I barely knew what had just happened, but I was so afraid. I knew I had to get out of there, fast. I ran home and hid in my closet, crying hysterically, and trembling. My brother, who was responsible for watching me, came home furious because I had left the store without him. He pulled me from the closet by my shirt, snarled at me, spitting out angry words and beating me with his fist.

My brother had no idea what had happened to me in the department store restroom, and I wasn't going to tell him. I didn't tell anyone.

That was the beginning of the nightmare of my life. Before the attack in the men's room, I was an A student. After the attack, I ended up flunking the third grade. My parents pulled me out of public school and put me into Catholic school, thinking it would help. My parents had no idea the torment I was going through. The bullying and abuse from my brother continued as well. When my dad reprimanded my brother for hitting me, he would beat me even worse, in our bedroom.

I carried my secret for several years, living in fear. In 1978, when I was thirteen and a freshman in high school, I was with my best friend when we saw police cars surrounding his house. Peeking through closed curtains, we also noticed news cameras. My friend's dad, who was a Chicago police officer, called to tell his wife, "There's something going on in our neighborhood. Don't let the kids leave the house!"

She turned on the news and the photograph of John Wayne Gacy came up on the screen. I knew he was the man who raped me and threatened to kill me several years earlier.

John Wayne Gacy, Jr. was an American serial killer and rapist who sexually assaulted and murdered at least thirty-three teenage boys and young men between 1972 and 1978. He was convicted of thirty-three murders and sentenced for twelve of these killings. He was executed in May, 1994. Now, John Wayne Gacy's case has been reopened after the discovery of eight more bodies. I am finally speaking out about what happened to me at the hands of this crazy murderer, and my story has been widely publicized in the Chicago area.

Technically, looking back, if he had killed me, I would have been his first victim. The feelings of guilt and shame, plus the ill treatment I have always received from my brother, caused me to attempt suicide seven years ago. It wasn't until I left my family that I could begin to recover from everything I'd gone through.

Did your brother ever say why he hated you?

Yes. He hated me because I was the youngest, and my mom always told everyone I was her favorite. It hurt him to hear these words coming from his own mother, and he resented me for it. She had done that my entire life. Even after I left the family, she would tell my brothers and sisters that I was her favorite. My mother had terminal cancer, so I arranged to see her once a week. I never went to her house because of the threats of my brother. We either met at my house or we went to a restaurant or a coffee shop.

Oh, it's great that you still had her. When she passed away you probably had a hard time going to the funeral.

I couldn't miss my mother's funeral. I had to hire a bodyguard to protect me from my brother.

What do you want to say to kids who have problems with bullies?

I want to educate kids that they need to come forward and not hide. The bullying they are suffering is not their fault. It's got to be people like me who have been through it who can show them that they are not alone and they can also get through it.

I'm a survivor, and they can survive this, too.

Section Four

Bullying Because of Race

"With ignorance comes fear—from fear comes bigotry. Education is the key to acceptance."

~Kathleen Patel, author of *The Bullying Epidemic: The Guide to Arm You for the Fight*

The Discrimination Never Ends
by Keesha Parsons

Keesha Parsons is the CEO of Mesonista.com - Fashion Style Guide and can be contacted via email at parsons@mesonista.com

***

I am an educated black woman in the business world. The discrimination never ends. It may be covered up a little better, but it's always there. In the working world, I was passed up for raises while everyone else received a raise and I had to ask my boss to speak up for me. I worked with supervisors who had less education and job experience than me. They would try to intimidate me and pick on me because of their higher position. With all these uncomfortable situations, I still revert back to my childhood for the most painful experience.

I grew up in a black neighborhood in Brooklyn, New York. Most of the families in my neighborhood were black. And most of my friends were black.

Even though I'm black, I was not born in the U.S. It wasn't until the principal called the students that were born overseas to her office that the other students knew I was raised in another culture. The discrimination from the African-American students began in my neighborhood and at school when the kids found out I was not American, but of Jamaican decent. On a daily basis, they began to mock my accent and tell me to go back to Jamaica.

I started work at a young age, so although my neighborhood was mostly African-American, my work friends were Caucasian, and I associated with them more than those in my neighborhood. My Caucasian co-workers were more interested to learn of my culture and food.

I had a major crush on this guy in high school. When I had a crush on someone, I would follow them around; don't ask why. So finally one day I had my white friend go and tell him that I liked him. I asked her what he said, and she told me he didn't say anything. We then assumed he didn't hear her. So she invited him over to her girl/boy party, which was mixed with both black and white friends. We even rigged 7 Minutes of Heaven so I could have some alone time with him and finally tell him how much I liked him. I ran to the closet and held the door open for him to enter and he took his sweet time, but, of course, with puppy love I didn't think much of it. He finally made it to the closet and whispered in my ear, "I don't date black girls." He then pushed past me and left the party. The way he looked at me made me question my self-worth for the first time ever. It was then that I began to see the world differently because of the color of my skin.

Did you view education as a way to rise above discrimination? How has education helped you?

Yes, a white woman with a high school diploma is more likely to receive a job offer than a black woman with a high school diploma. That motivated me to work harder to ensure that I would have the needed credentials for the job market. With my experience in the legal field coupled with my graduate degree, I was placed on top of the pile for job offers, beating out those with lesser experience and fewer degrees. I was hired as an administrator of patents and trademarks. However, the issue did arise that many white and black workers were insulted that I got the job, and even tried to sabotage my position when they realized that I made more money than they did. They didn't understand how I could have more experience because I was younger than most of my colleagues. Even supervisors with lesser degrees attempted to hold back my raise or give me a hard time because of my salary. It's a double edged sword: at one point, the employers found me to be an asset to the company, but, because of their own insecurities, many white co-workers and supervisors believed that a black woman should not be above them and making more money than them.

Where do you live now?

Long Island, New York

What would your advice be to others who are experiencing discrimination at school or at work?

My advice is to be secure in your person and remain strong and realize that there will always be people against you who try to stop you. Never let another's view of you get in the way of your goals. Stay focused.

My grandmother always told me, "Anything and anyone who is against you is only a distraction. Keep focused on your goals, your dreams, and always put God first."

Sometimes you have to dig deep for that inner strength and sometimes you will cry, but keep fighting and never give up on you; don't allow someone to tell you what you're worth. God created you, and only God is above you.

***

"Those who hurt others will also hurt themselves."
~Natsuki Takaya

Our Slanted Eyes
by Chinee and Sunhee Park

Chinee and Sunhee Park are celebrity psychics and stars of the TV show
Twintuition

***

When our Korean mother gave birth to us, a set of female twins, she already had two girls around the ages of four and five years old. Our Korean father, a professional boxer, wanted boys, so he divorced her and left her with no money. Our birth mother worked as a hairdresser and couldn't afford four small girls. She had no choice but to put us up for adoption. We were taken to the orphanage at the age of two. We have no recollection of being in the adoption agency, but apparently the agency caught on fire and I, Chinhee, was caught in the fire. I still have a scar from it. But there are no records of us; therefore, we cannot get any validation.

Our adoptive parents lived in a small town in upstate New York. Our adoptive mother, an Irish woman who was thirty-five years old, and our adoptive father, a forty-eight-year-old Italian man, were trying to have children, but she was infertile. They had tried adoption in the U.S., but waited years for a child because of the age of our father. She wrote of her dilemma to the newspaper columnist, Ann Landers, who is also a twin.

Ann Landers wrote back in the column and told her that adoption in the U.S. was difficult due to all the abortions performed each year. She suggested for the hopeful couple to adopt overseas, and gave her the address to our Korean orphanage. Our parents contacted the orphanage, requesting one boy. They went through the process and waited for a child. The Korean agency sent them a photo of my sister and me. The agency made us look like boys, told them we were twins, and they could not separate us. Our parents took one look at our photo and said, yes, they wanted us.

When our adoptive parents met us at JFKNYC airport, they realized that we were twin girls. Because my parents were getting older and they had waited so long to adopt, they took us anyway. Our gender didn't seem as important anymore once they saw us.

Our Korean names are Chinhee and Sunhee, but our American parents changed our names to Lisa and Lori. Life was good with them in the beginning, but it turned sour for us when our father started sexually abusing us at the age of five. When Sunhee told our mother about the abuse, our mother beat her because she didn't believe it. We quickly learned that we would never have the support of our mother.

What is it like for you being of Korean decent, living in America?

Chinhee: We were raised in upstate New York in a pretty much all-white neighborhood. There was one black family and one Asian family that we knew of. We were constantly made fun of. People would do the slanted-eye thing with their hands and make fun of our eyes because we were different looking. Because we're twins, two Korean girls stuck out like sore thumbs in our white, Catholic, suburban neighborhood. Back then it was so hard for us, but now we think it's beautiful to be different.

Sunhee: My sister, Chinhee, would get beaten up getting off the school bus. Then one day she said enough, and she just finally ended up beating the guy back with her book bag. That was the confrontation that helped my sister to stop getting beaten up.

What about your parents? Did they help you when you were having trouble?

Chinhee: No, we didn't have much support. When I look back on that incident, I would have handled it differently, but I already knew I didn't have the support of my mother, so I didn't think I'd get the support of other people. I should have handled the situation another way, but the only solution I could think of was to give it back to him. My bag was so full of books, I actually put the kid in the hospital. My mother dragged me to the hospital to see him and apologize. I looked straight at his mother and I said, "I'm not apologizing for beating him up because your son has been beating me up and making fun of me for the past three months."

His mother was livid with him. I actually got more support from his mother than my own mother. It was crazy.

I had a lot of problems, and no help for them from my mother. I'd go into my creative mode and just draw anything and everything. So my creative outlet was what saved me. My sister was too busy doing her own thing in her own bedroom, so we really didn't communicate much. It's hard to support each other when you both have the same issue.

Did you have friends who wouldn't bully you?

Chinhee: Yes, we had friends. My bullying experience was in grade school. In the seventh grade, we went to a new school with new kids.

That's when it turned around for us. We became the most popular kids in school. I was elected president of my class, while Sunhee was elected secretary.

I'll bet you didn't bully anybody, did you?

Sunhee: No, we were friends with everybody. We were nice to everybody. We were kind. It's really weird, but the bullying didn't make a negative impact on us. It made us stronger inside, which made us appreciate life. It made us better people.

Chinhee: I would always see a person in the cafeteria alone and I would make them feel better and invite the person to come and sit with us. If I ever saw someone getting bullied, I would try to break it up and stop it. I would always try to help the kids who looked depressed and looked like they were having a hard time being accepted.

Did the sexual abuse continue into high school?

Chinhee: The sexual abuse ended when I was around thirteen. I made myself so busy that he wouldn't do it again and I yelled at him.

Sunhee: I told you that our mother wasn't supportive of us. She was in her own world and she denied everything. But we never talked to each other about it until we were much older. Back then, our household was so dysfunctional that it was like we barely knew each other.

It was kind of hard to communicate because we were both being abused. I escaped by being busy with sports and just being out of the house all day and all night. It was my own way of dealing and coping. My sister would go out and party and do things with her friends and then sleep a lot. She had to sleep more to get over the stuff.

Even before the adoption, our mother had begun a battle with cancer. The cancer was in remission, and when we were twelve or thirteen, the cancer came back. It all went downhill when she began abusing the drugs she was on for pain. It changed her to a mean person. She was very abusive verbally and physically. My sister and I became punching bags for our parents, and often wondered why they bothered to adopt us.

When your mom was so ill, did household responsibilities such as cooking and cleaning fall on you both?

Chinhee: Yes, we had to grow up fast. It was quite overwhelming and stressful to have to take care of our mother, do our homework, go to volleyball and soccer practice, games, and tournaments, and still try to be kids. I was not able to handle it all. Sunhee ended up taking care of our mother more. I had to be away from her and out of the house in order to keep my sanity. She was very abusive on her morphine, and

Sunhee was her little slave.

Our mother died when we were fifteen.

When your mother died, did your grandmother or an aunt come to help out?

Chinhee: They offered their help and condolences, but we pretty much pushed them away. We disconnected from everyone—family, friends, and even each other. It was a rough time, and that was the only way we could cope with the abuse and loss. Looking back, we always knew we had the love of our extended family. They didn't know about all the abuse that we were going through.

Sunhee was always a straight A student. She was on high honor roll a lot. I started off good, made honor roll a few times, but then went down to average after Mom died.

After we left our dysfunctional home, we started to use our Korean names, and we believe our spiritual gifts come from our Korean heritage. Chinhee, in Korean, means "Big Heart," and Sunhee means "Full of Life." We also wanted to disconnect from our American names and bad memories. Using our Korean names helped us connect with our true selves and heal from a lot of wounds.

We don't mind you bringing up our sexuality, as we are more than proud and adamant to inspire others in the closet to be proud of who they are. We no longer live in fear and don't want others to. The more we all stand proud together, the more we overcome our fears and don't feel scared to live our lives. We came out publicly in our interview with this brand-new magazine *BelleSprit* and we have another upcoming interview with *The Advocate*, the world's largest gay publication. So we do not mind at all. In fact, we encourage you to mention that part of us, since it's a very large part of who we are and we are not ashamed of it.

***

"There's no race, no religion, no class system, no color, nothing, no sexual orientation that makes us better than anyone else. We are all deserving of love."

~Sandra Bullock

Section Five

Bullied Because of a Disability

"What if the kid you bullied at school, grew up, and turned out to be the only surgeon who could save your life?"

~Lynette Mather

Celebrities with Disabilities

Beethoven was a deaf composer best known for Beethoven's 5th symphony.

Nicholas Brendon, an actor best known for his part on *Buffy the Vampire Slayer*, suffered from stuttering.

Ray Charles was a singer and performer who was visually impaired.

Albert Einstein was a famous scientist and author of the Law of Relativity. He suffered from dyslexia and ADD.

Stephen Hawking, a world-famous scientist and the author of *Brief History in Time*, has been bound to a wheelchair and has a simulated voice due to Lou Gehrig's Disease.

James Earl Jones is an actor best known for his famous voice as Darth Vader in *Star Wars* and the voice of Mufasa in Disney's *The Lion King*. He had to work hard to overcome a stutter.

Helen Keller was born deaf and blind. She was taught to speak and spell letters with her hands. Along with her teacher, Miss Sullivan, Helen gave lectures to raise money for the American Foundation for the Blind.

Robert Kennedy, U.S. Senator, was learning disabled and had ADD.

John Lennon, a musician and a singer/songwriter for the Beatles, was learning disabled and had ADD.

Marlee Matlin is an actress who is hearing impaired. She is best known for her role in *Children of a Lesser God*.

Marilyn Monroe has been gone for many years, but we still see this actress on posters, T-shirts, and even coffee mugs. Well known for her part in *The Seven Year Itch*, Marilyn suffered with a stuttering problem and depression.

Franklin Delano Roosevelt was the thirty-second president of the United States. He had polio, but he hid his disability so well that millions of Americans never knew he was bound to a wheelchair.

Robin Williams, comedian and actor, suffered from a learning disability and ADD.

Stevie Wonder is a visually impaired singer/performer.

***

"Never say you can't. Thinking you can't will always hold you back from doing the things you can!"

~Timothy Pina, *Bullying Ben*

Don't Quit Until You're on Top
by Donna Hill

Donna Hill is an advocate for accessibility and inclusion of blind people in society, and author of The Heart of Applebutter Hill

***

I was born legally blind from a degenerative eye condition called retinitis pigmentosa. As the first legally blind person mainstreamed in my school district, I was bullied throughout my public school years. Nowadays, I work as an advocate for those who have blindness-related issues and have heard stories of bullying from other blind people.

I was legally blind primarily due to the field loss. I had some reading vision, which pretty much disappeared altogether between my senior year of high school and my freshman year of college. As the years went on, I continued to lose more vision. I still have a small amount of light perception, but I can no longer hold a black shirt and a white one up to the light and tell which one is darker. However, I still enjoy daylight and have a strong visual memory/imagination.

Going to Public School

I started school in the first grade (we didn't have kindergarten in our district at the time). Although I was the first legally blind student in the school, the teacher gave no explanation of my condition to the other students, and I was not given any formal help.

The theory was that, "If she wants to come to public school, she can learn like everyone else." I flunked math in third grade because the teacher wrote the problems on a part of the blackboard I couldn't see from my seat in the front row. I thought for months that the vocabulary words on the board near me were all there was.

In sixth grade, a "sight-saving" teacher from the county pulled me from class once a week for special one-on-one lessons which were held in the teachers' restroom. The only thing of value I can remember was the puzzle map of the USA, which had each state as a separate piece. It gave me an understanding of our country that I wish I'd had of Europe, Asia, and Africa, et cetera.

The Nature of the Bullying

The bullying began on day one of first grade. It started out verbal, but became physical. Kids would throw my books to watch me struggle to find them, or hit me and run away.

I did have friends who were nice to me when no one else was around. One boy, the son of my piano teacher, stood up for me in fifth grade and the kids began targeting him because of his help.

Early on, I mentioned my problems to my parents, and we talked quite a lot about it. They couldn't believe people would be that cruel. They tried to give me coping skills like "Just ignore them" or "Ask them how they'd like it if someone did that to them." Eventually, I realized that nothing I could do or not do helped in the slightest and that my parents were not equipped to deal with it, so I stopped mentioning it.

My teachers and principal usually looked the other way. Some gave lip service to the idea that the kids shouldn't do that, but there were no repercussions, no outreach to me to help me deal with it. Some teachers—my third-grade teacher comes to mind—thought it was funny. Some resented having me in their class. My fifth grade teacher held me up as a way to shame the class. "If Donna, with her problems, can get an A, why can't you?" This didn't endear me to my classmates.

The bullying escalated as I got older, and I would blow up every two years and end up in the principal's office. I was suspended in high school for being in a fight with another girl who had been bullying me all year.

My problem with bullying continued right up to high school graduation.

Now there are organizations like the National Organization of Parents of Blind Children that are very active in helping parents get their children the education to which they are entitled. Kids whose parents are in these groups meet other blind kids and have a sense that they aren't alone.

What would you like to say to kids who are being bullied because of a disability?

What's happening to you is wrong, and you don't deserve it. I'm sure it feels like you are alone in this, but many of us have had to deal with it. Unfortunately, it is the outgrowth of what society believes about blindness. They're wrong; you can do anything you put your mind to, and you deserve the chance to pursue your education and your dreams in peace. Some of us are working to change things, and there is far more progress than you may realize. Blind people are already excelling in almost any field you can imagine, including engineering, chemistry, journalism, law, and many other fields. A couple of blind guys graduated from medical school. To succeed, you need the proper tools and training and a can-do attitude.

Your parents are probably at a loss as to how to handle this; they're learning about these issues right along with you. Encourage them to find someone to help them. I recommend the National Federation of the Blind and the National Organization of Parents of Blind Children. Check to see if you have a state affiliate. There are other groups as well. The important thing is to find people who will believe in you. Be brave and don't give up. When you get discouraged, let yourself have a little time to deal with the way you feel, but don't allow yourself to dwell on it for long. Don't quit until you're on top!

***

"Because even the smallest of words can be the ones to hurt you, or save you."

~Natsuki Takaya

Breaking Down Barriers
by Chris Hendricks

Lead singer of the Chris Hendricks Band and speaker for the band's anti-bullying program, Breaking Down Barriers. You can find Chris's album Noise on iTunes. "Our music is very motivational and very positive. We don't curse in the music and there are no inappropriate lyrics, so it can be available to people of any age."

Chris was born with cerebral palsy and was severely bullied as a child because of his disability. But with the help of his voice and guitar, he turned his disability into an opportunity to share his experience with and provide inspiration for others facing a similar situation. The band visits schools in the North Carolina area to present their Breaking Down Barriers anti- bullying program.

***

Chris, I understand that you have cerebral palsy. What kind of difficulties has this disability created for you?

I've had trouble walking since the age of four. I've been in and out of a wheelchair, I get fatigued very easily, and my gait, the way I walk, is a bit abnormal, among other things. Those are the biggest problems, I'd say.

Many people with your disability aren't able to walk. It's great that you can walk.

I got really lucky with that. Doctors told me early on that I wouldn't be able to walk. So far, so good. I do have braces on my legs, but I am walking now completely. I do use a cane, but the cane's more of a style thing.

So did you realize right away that you were different than other children around you?

It didn't really hit me until I went to kindergarten. In elementary school, kids were curious about my braces and they would ask me a lot of questions. They were very friendly and concerned about me. Going to school really wasn't intimidating to me until middle school and high school. In the upper grades, I noticed a lot of fear in my colleagues' eyes. Their reaction also made me fearful. I had a tendency to shy away from kids and focus more on my school work rather than my social life.

Were these different kids than you went to elementary school with?

Yes, they were. I went to a public elementary school, and in middle school and high school my mom wanted me to get a better education, so she put me in a private Catholic school.

How did kids in your school make your life difficult?

They would trip me, push me around, and shove me into the lockers. What's interesting to me is that the physical abuse wasn't as painful as the ignorance and ignoring my presence. Like I said before, the largest emotional toll for me was just seeing how afraid everyone else was.

Were they calling you names?

Oh, yeah, yeah. I was called crippled, and actually that was really harsh. Some people even called me retarded. Kids used to tease me by calling me the Terminator. Nowadays I've turned that around and I use the name Terminator as a positive thing.

Did you have some close friends?

I had one really close friend in middle school. His name was A. J. and he stuck with me when no one else wanted to be my friend. We were great friends. In high school I had a couple friends here and there, but for the most part, my social circle was pretty small compared to a lot of kids in my high school.

Did you have any teachers who would help you or make it so other kids would understand what was going on with you?

The teachers I had in middle school and high school were wonderful people, but they really overcompensated. Even though they were trying to help, they really made it worse. In middle school if I needed to go to the restroom, rather than letting me go by myself, they would make me go with another student. Of course, that was really humiliating. It's amazing how little people understand about disabilities.

When did you start singing?

I started singing when I was four years old, which is the same year I was diagnosed with my condition. When I was really young, I was a member of the North Carolina Boys Choir. In middle school and high school, I sang for talent shows, but I didn't actually start a band until college. My first band was called The Rising.

I'm actually a professional recording artist now and I tour all around the U.S. with The Chris Hendricks Band. We just got back from Los

Angeles, Dallas, and Baltimore. Most recently we opened for a band called Delta Ray, which was just featured on *The Jay Leno Show* and interviewed in *Rolling Stone Magazine*. It was very exciting, and our proudest accomplishment to date.

I understand that you put on an anti-bullying program for schools.

Actually, the band and I go around to different middle schools and high schools and we perform for the kids. We play a set of songs of original rock music, and then I tell them my story about how I was picked on in middle school and high school. I like to tell kids about how I was able to use the bullying as fuel to recreate myself and become a recording artist. My success with music has generated a lot of confidence for me in my adult life. Our Breaking Down Barriers anti-bullying program has been a positive experience for us and the kids.

Can you tell me a little bit about what you say to the kids?

Sure. I talk about how being different is not a problem. I tell them how being unique can be used as a really powerful tool. Marching to the beat of your own drum is really what people are looking for because it makes life interesting. Kids in middle school and high school shouldn't be afraid of kids who are different. They don't know who the person they're picking on is going to become. Everyone has so much potential at such a young age, and it would be a shame to stomp that out by picking on them.

What is the response from the kids?

The response has been tremendous. There are actually online videos of the kids standing up and cheering or screaming. They really get into our music, and love dancing around. We've had some incidences after our performances and speeches where bullies have broken down and apologized to the kids they'd been picking on. In some schools, teachers have generated classroom discussions around the issues brought up in my Breaking Down Barriers talk.

I'd like to think that it has brought the level of bullying down at the schools we've visited. I don't know that for certain, but the vibes I get are definitely positive.

Do you have a message you would like to give kids who are being bullied?

You can realize your own potential by searching out your own personal passion in life. For me, it's music, singing, and performing. When you're young, you have so much time to explore and find out what makes you unique. Particularly for kids with disabilities, I'd say rather than looking at your differences as a hindrance, really look at them as a gift. Find out what advantages they can give you and what artistic and creative outlets your disability can generate.

Just to hammer the point home, vulnerability is strength. A lot of times, kids are afraid of their own potential. You just need to realize that each of us was brought into the world with a purpose. The sooner you realize that, the more positive you are going to become, and you will have a real positive adulthood.

***

"The good news is nothing ever is permanent. You are the artist of your life...so take your brush & paint it bright!"

~Timothy Pina, *Bullying Ben*

How My Son Triumphed Over Bullying
by Victoria Marin

Victoria is the author of Aiden's Waltz, www.aidenswaltz.com

***

I would like to share my son's story of how he triumphed over bullying through the art of ballroom dancing.

Targeting His Differences

During Aiden's fifth year of school, his peers as well as his general education teacher targeted him and made him feel quite different. When he was a member of the town's recreational basketball team, he was told by the other boys that he was only on the team to give the "good players" a rest. Aiden would use words and phrases incorrectly in text messages when he talked to kids in his class at school. Because of his problem with spelling, he received many vulgar text message replies from the other boys. They told him he couldn't play with the other boys because he was stupid. One afternoon, a much larger boy followed Aiden out from school and wrestled him to the ground, giving him a bruised shoulder.

Aiden's disability made it difficult for him to achieve success in the classroom. He was the last to be chosen for group projects and was often the scapegoat when things went awry. He was also excluded from playground activities and play. While boys and girls gathered in groups at the lunch tables, Aiden sat alone. The boys from his class would steal the special treats I would send in his lunch, call him a loser, and then return to their friends and ignore Aiden.

The school conducted their own evaluations, and their school psychologist met with Aiden on a number of occasions. I was told he was dyslexic and possibly had a general processing disorder. He had an IEP evaluation with recommendations for replacement classes for Language Arts and Reading.

Set Up to Fail

The most unfortunate part of my son's story was that his teacher also became one of the bullies. The child study team was involved, and she was aware that Aiden had a problem with organizational skills. He often misplaces papers. I had a system put in place with different binders and notebooks to help him be organized in school, but he would still misplace worksheets. She would admittedly refuse him extra copies and basically set him up to fail because he would not be prepared with his homework. The next day, his teacher would call Aiden to the front of the class and ask him for the homework she knew he didn't have.

One day I sent in a bag of veggie chips for his classroom snack. I don't know if he was chewing loudly or if the bag was too loud, but she had him go up in front of the class and throw them into the garbage can.

On the day of the winter concert, when I decided to stay and help organize his locker, I finally found out about the extent of the bullying. One of the students came out into the hallway and said to me, "You know, the teacher yells at Aiden every day. She yells at him in front of the classroom." That's when I called him aside and found out that he would raise his hand to ask questions in class and she would refuse to answer him. When he would try to ask another student, she would yell at him for speaking in class.

Academically, my son was set up to fail. This bullying led to a breakdown where he refused to enter the school building. His verbal communication and eye contact had become minimal.

Home Schooling Was the Answer

After months of meeting with the child study team, his teacher, the principal, and the superintendent, no action was taken to change Aiden's classroom or to improve his experiences at school. I made the decision to withdraw him from the school. At that time, he was a C student at best. I enrolled him in Red Oak Academy, an online school that holds virtual classes. There is a live teacher who appears via webcam; with the use of a smart board, she can write notes or send links to sites to enhance her lecture.

Without the fear and anxiety of the school weighing on his mind, his grades improved to A's and B's. Aiden was no longer afraid of his teacher, and when he asked questions in his online school, he received answers. This led to an enriched learning experience. The bullies were no longer a part of his day.

I have five children and the youngest is eighteen months old. I quit my job as an occupational therapist to stay home with my children and give Aiden the help he needed. Having Aiden at home helped me to see many of the subtle signs and symptoms that my son was having. I took him to see a specialist and was told that he had Asperger's, which is a form of autism. Prior to that, I worked full time and he was in school and child care. Therefore, I did not see the signs.

The Symptoms of Asperger's

Aiden lacked social skills, especially knowing when to take turns when talking during a conversation. He had trouble making friends and maintaining relationships. Not only did he misuse words and phrases, he often didn't understand the meanings of them, especially in the context of a joke or sarcasm. He avoided eye contact except with those with whom he was very comfortable. Aiden is extremely knowledgeable about animals and wildlife, and would often have one-sided conversations about this topic. I also noticed he would move his head and upper body in a wavelike fashion until someone called attention to it, and then he would stop.

Ballroom Dancing

At the same time I withdrew Aiden from school, I enrolled him in ballroom dancing lessons. The components of ballroom dancing helped him to overcome his social and emotional challenges. He had to maintain eye contact and verbally communicate with his dance partner. Ballroom dancing is taught in a way that meets the learning styles of most children with special needs. The steps are taught one at a time, and there is repetition. Mastery of each step is completed before a new one is introduced. In Aiden's case, he responds better to one-step directives rather than multi-steps. Because he was placed in a leadership role on the dance floor, his self-esteem and confidence improved. He was no longer hesitant to participate in group activities. I am proud to share that he recently danced his first cha-cha in front of an audience of approximately thirty people!

My Mission

This experience has led me on a mission to educate parents of children with special needs about the power of dance. For children who prefer not to be touched or have people within close proximity, ballroom dance helps to increase their tolerance as partners maintain close proximity to one another. The rhythmic movements can help to increase muscle tone, while classical music is beneficial for brain health and the organization of internal and external information. Ballroom dancing provides a multisensory approach to managing the symptoms of autism and other varying types of diagnoses along the spectrum.

I wish to bring ballroom dance as an option to families, as dance is empowering and encourages pride and joy in children with disabilities.

Every kid with a disability should know that we each have our own form of disability. For example, I struggle with mathematics. This is my disability. You are not different because of your disability; you are special and you have the talents and abilities to achieve success.

Note to parents: The prevalence of bullying of children with special needs is far greater than we know. These children are easy targets for the bullies. I urge parents of children with special needs to be aware of the non-verbal signs of bullying. Thankfully, my son found his ability in ballroom dance and was able to overcome the effects of his bullying.

***

"They have all these laws and social boundaries to keep them in check. The problem is villains and bullies just ignore that kind of thing."
~Charles deLint, *Little (Grrl) Lost*

Fighting to Survive with a Disability
by Mark Horner

Mark is the author of Consistently Persistent: Living with the Tourette Trifecta.

***

I was born with Tourette's, ADHD, and OCD. Unfortunately, they didn't know what I had until I was forty-three years old. Since I have all three of these, I have coined the phrase Tourette's Trifecta. I have three separate medical conditions which made me an easy target for bullies.

Seventy percent of the people with Tourette's have ADD, ADHD, OCD, or a combination of the three, so it's not uncommon. The problem is that the condition involves involuntary tics. A kid with Tourette's will do things that other kids don't understand. I would twitch my nose, my mouth, my left shoulder, or any number of parts of my body. With Tourette's, there are two types of tics. There's a motor tic, like I was just describing, and there's a vocal tic. Screaming, shouting, snorting, or nonstop talking are all symptoms of Tourette's. But these are by no means the only vocal tics associated with Tourette's. Unfortunately, I didn't know what was wrong. I didn't know why I behaved like that.

Kids can be unmercifully cruel, and that's what they were doing to me. Besides having an unknown disability, it didn't help that I was physically small and my last name is Horner. Now that I'm grown, I'm still only five-four, but I now weigh two hundred pounds and I am built like a human fire hydrant. But, of course, I was much smaller when I was in high school. The teasing continued through elementary, junior high, and high school.

I also grew up in a rough neighborhood. The southeast quadrant of Dallas is called Pleasant Grove, and it's one of the roughest sections of the city. I mean gangs, violence, drugs, you name it. All of these things made for a very hard upbringing. The fact that my father was a violent alcoholic, my mother was an addict, and my younger brother was both didn't make my life any easier. I was pretty much on my own. No one at home ever asked me about my homework, and my parents didn't care if I had dinner, took a bath, or had clean clothes for school.

The problems at home only compounded my problems at school. My brother was openly gay and came out of the closet at the age of fifteen. Even though I wasn't gay, I got treated like I was. I was called names and got beat up on a regular basis. You can imagine what kind of social life I had. Once in a while, I'd find somebody who was a friend for a little while. But after he found out about my reputation, he didn't want to have anything to do with me.

There were a couple of boys in the neighborhood who were two years older than me. I thought they were my friends, but when I was about thirteen, they cornered me in one of their houses during the day, attacked me, and forced me to do sexual things against my will.

I didn't know I could be called so many different nicknames, anything from "Rabbit," "Twitch," and "Bugs" to "Shaky." There were a few other names I'd rather not remember.

It was hard to go to school, but I didn't have much choice in the matter. I tried skipping school sometimes, but the risk of getting caught and dealing with my father put too much fear in me. I just went to school and had to grin and bear it. In high school, I couldn't date anyone from my part of town, because they all knew my reputation. I had to date someone from another part of town who didn't know anybody from Pleasant Grove.

Life After High School

I dropped out of high school halfway through my second time in the eleventh grade. I couldn't keep going to school just to endure the bullying and name-calling, coupled with my parents and brother being addicts. The emotional pain was by far the worst. Physical pain will heal. Emotional pain will stay with you for years and years and years. I survived just for the fact that I refused to be knocked down and kept down.

After I quit high school, I went into an apprentice program to become a machinist, and eventually they got tired of me, even though I had no idea what I was doing that bothered them. Next I decided to go into the Navy. I was thinking that maybe if I got away, it would help, but it didn't. It actually made my situation worse. People who have Tourette's tend to have very high IQs. I like to think for myself, and the military frowns on that. I was discharged from the Navy after three years. The official reason for my discharge was "unable to adapt to military life."

I got out of the Navy and started drifting from job to job. It was always the same. "Markus, we like you. You're smart, you're loyal, and you work harder than anybody here, but you just don't fit in."

I've had jobs that only lasted one day. Other jobs have lasted two, three, four days, or a week. From the age of sixteen to forty-three I was fired over two hundred times. When I found a part-time job as a night marketer for RCA, I seemed to fit in. I managed to keep this job for two years. The only reason they could tolerate me was because we were only working three hours a day, and my production was so high they couldn't justify firing me. I set five national sales records for RCA. I've never been fired for lack of ability, or lack of talent. It was always the same thing: "You don't fit in."

My number one problem with OCD is being a perfectionist. I am extremely perfectionistic, to the point that I drive people crazy. I would give the job everything I had and I would expect the people around me to do the same. Well, they're not going to do that. My work record makes others look bad, and when that happens, they start complaining. Eventually the boss has to do something to restore peace, and that usually means, "Mark, here are your walking papers."

You know, I actually had a girlfriend break up with me because she couldn't keep up with me.

I said, "Kathy, who asked you to keep up with me?"

She said, "Well, your apartment is absolutely spotless, and everything is in order. It's absolutely perfect. I can't keep up with that."

"Well, you don't have to. Nobody is asking you to."

She left because it made her uncomfortable.

I'm a Survivor
Now that I'm older, I have been to a therapist more times than I can remember. Approximately one month before I was diagnosed with Tourette's, the psychiatrist that I was seeing came in and just plopped down in his chair. I could tell that something was bothering him.

I said, "What's the matter, Doc?"

He said, "Markus, I've been treating you for two years now and I still don't know what's going on. The problem is that the symptoms of each of the illnesses mask the symptoms of the other two, so it's hard to isolate one from another." Then he said, "Markus, I'm going to tell you this. You have a will to survive like I have never seen before in my thirty years of practice. If you were in a plane crash up in the mountains and everyone else on that plane was killed, you would be the one S.O.B. on that plane that refused to die. Ten days later, you would be the one to walk out of the mountains alive. Frostbit, but you would be breathing. That's just how determined you are not to give up."

He was right. I have no idea where it comes from, but I know it's there. I'm the kind of guy who refuses to stay down for the count. God knows I've been through enough.

How is your life now?
I'm married right now, for the second time. We have been married for twenty-five years. I'll tell you right now, there are times when I am

extremely difficult to be around. She puts up with it—I'm not sure how.

We have a daughter who is a twenty-two-year-old pre-med student. I have been told more times than I can remember what an outstanding father I am. My daughter told me that some of her teachers have said so; the parents of some of her friends have also said so. Even though my father was never there for me, I never found being a father all that difficult. I just use common sense, and it seems to work.

I have made a good life for myself and my family. I have owned my own handyman business for over twenty-five years. I'm also a freelance writer; I write a column for the Dallas Morning News, and I have written my memoir, titled *Consistently Persistent: Living with Tourette Trifecta*. I didn't know I had the ability to write until a couple of years ago.

What advice would you give kids who are being bullied because of physical disabilities?

Some bullying is physical, but most of it's verbal. A guy may get away with bullying me one time, but he won't get away with bullying me twice. I will stand there and look at him like I'm looking right through him. I won't respond to anything he says or does. When he gets through talking, I just turn around and walk away without saying a word. He's not going to get under my skin again, regardless of what names he calls me. Is it hard to stand there and stare him down? You bet it is.

If a group of people are threatening to harm you, turn around and run. Try to pick out a safe place where you can run to. If there is no safe place to run, you might have to bluff your way through. If there's only one attacker and there's nowhere to run, you may have to fight. But, should this happen, do everything you can to make him realize that you are not an easy target, and that you are going to do everything you can to hurt him.

I am now a second-degree black belt in karate. Becoming a black belt has taught me that no one ever wins in a street fight and that it's best to avoid fighting, if you can. Getting the black belt was far more for my self-confidence than anything else.

Section Six

Bullied Because of Religion

"It's always okay to do the right thing. It's never okay to be a bully."

~Magdalena VandenBerg

They Failed and I Overcame
by Paul Draper

Paul is a mentalist, anthropologist, public speaker, and host of Mysteries of the Mind

***

Paul, I understand you were bullied because you were Jewish and you were living in a community where most of the kids were Mormons.

I suffered a great deal of religious discrimination growing up as a Jew in Utah.

At what age did the discrimination begin?

The discrimination began very early, and I don't think the local population understood that what they were doing was discriminating, but it was clear what was going on. As early as the first grade, kids were told by their parents that they were only able to invite kids to their birthday party if the kids were in their ward. The LDS or Mormon Church congregation is called a ward. The kids would come down the aisles in the classroom with invitations asking, "What ward are you in? Here's an invitation." And because I was Jewish, they would say, "Oh, you can't come to my party."

Did you have good friends in school?

My closest friends were Muslims, Presbyterians, Seventh-day Adventists, and Lutherans, because we were the kids who weren't invited to anyone else's events. Who would have thought my best friend in the whole world would be Shahene Pezeshki, whose father's family came from Tehran, Iran. The kid with the Jewish background and the kid with the Muslim background became best friends in Utah in part because of religious discrimination. I'm not blaming Mormons, but wherever there's a majority, human beings are cruel. I don't mean to infer that Mormons, in and of themselves, are cruel. The meanest Jews in the world are the Jews in Israel. The meanest Muslims are the Muslims in Iran or Iraq. It could be that the meanest Baptists in the world are in Georgia.

Celebrating Jewish Holidays

Discrimination didn't only come from the students. When I was in grade school, there was a big poster in the hallway of the school which said, "Holladay Elementary School Wishes You a Merry Christmas." They stuck a picture of all the students on this poster. I went up to the principal and asked, "When are you going to put up a poster that says 'We Wish You a Happy Hanukkah' and put all the students' faces on that?"

The principal laughed at me, saying it was ludicrous.

I said, "I want my picture taken off that poster."

The principal said, "Don't you wish your fellow students a Merry Christmas?"

I said of course I did. "Don't they wish me a Happy Hanukkah?" I was the only Jewish kid in my school, so they weren't going to do anything for any Jewish holiday.

Starting in junior high school and continuing through college, I was docked a letter grade if I missed school for the Jewish High Holidays. I had high school teachers who told me, when we were on a choir trip, that we had to stay in our hotel room and have LDS general conference on the television screen, even if we didn't watch it. Then in college, when I ran for student body president for my university, they printed in the student newspaper that my opponent was a returned missionary and an active member of the LDS Church; then for me they wrote, "Paul Draper is a Jew." They stated this clearly in the paper, even though our religion had nothing to do with our politics.

If you're in Utah and you are an LDS, Caucasian, middle class, male, then life is pretty good and you won't think there's any discrimination in the world. But if you're anything other than that, it can be pretty rough. One time in grade school, I had a kid shove me down the stairs and call me a Christ killer. It was really harsh, but it made me have a thick skin.

Luckily for me, Judaism is something that can be hidden, if one wants. Later in life, it came to a point where girls wouldn't date me because they were only allowed to date people who were LDS. The argument was "Why date someone you're not going to marry? Why date someone who can't go to heaven?"

Did your whole family suffer from discrimination in your neighborhood?

We certainly had fear of it. In Judaism, one of the things you are supposed to do is put a Mezuzah outside your door and a Menorah with lights in your window at Hanukkah time. My mom felt pressured not to do those things and she would hide her Judaism for fear of reactions in the community. There were times when we'd find nasty stuff written on our sidewalk, or offensive pamphlets in our mailbox. What's funny is that half of my linage is LDS, and half of our family is Jewish. I just happen to be practicing in the Jewish half. It's really too bad we weren't treated better.

Did your parents sit you down and talk to you about the problems you were going through?

Not really. They mostly said, "Don't cause trouble. Don't let people know." For all of junior high and high school I decided to start wearing the Star of David necklace on the outside of my shirt. I was going to be the best Jew I could possibly be, and I was going to represent Judaism. I also decided the reason people hated Jews was because they'd never met one. If I was an exemplary member of the faith, people would remember me. Down the road, when anyone mentioned a Jewish person, I wanted them to think, *I knew Paul, and he wasn't so bad.* From then on, it became a mission of mine to be a great person and represent the faith. What a difficult task for a kid. I'm glad now that I made that decision. Now that I live in Vegas, I'm not so adamant about letting people know I'm Jewish. We make up a much larger percentage of the population here and it isn't as big of an issue so I no longer feel it is as necessary.

Did any of your teachers step in and help you in any way?

It was really the opposite most of the time. I had a lot more teachers who tried to convert me to Mormonism. In junior high school, a teacher asked me, "Paul, how many Jews do you think there are in the world?" I didn't know, but I said a number that was kind of small. He laughed at me and the class laughed with him. Then he told the class how many Jews died in the holocaust and that there are about thirteen million Jews left on the earth today. That seemed like such a large number when I was growing up as the only Jew in my school.

I had another teacher in junior high tell me that Jesus was going to come back in the year 2000 and I needed to repent before he did.

There was a great organization called the National Conference of Christians and Jews. They held summer camps and diversity initiatives. It later became the National Conference of Community and Justice. In Utah, it's known by the name of Inclusion Center, and has an office on the University of Utah campus. I began actively participating in their leadership camps at the end of junior high. The camps dealt with bigotry and racism through education, advocacy, and leadership initiatives. They're really a great group. They have helped me throughout my life, so even when I was running for student government at Weber State University, I held a Passover service in the diversity center. I thought that a Passover service was something that could be a gift to the community for people to see what it is Jews do and celebrate. Because Passover is the story of the Exodus, it's not only a part of Judaism, but it's also a part of Christian theology. Judaism has no intention of conversion. We don't have missionaries.

The members of the LDS Institute came over with tape measures in the middle of my service and put tape marks on the ground for the distance from the polls to my table to make sure that I wasn't in violation to the rules by being too close to the polling place while doing this interfaith service in the diversity center.

During college elections, there was a rule that you couldn't campaign or put up posters off campus, so I wasn't allowed to put up posters at the local coffee shop or a music store. But the one and only debate was going to be held at the LDS Institute, which was clearly off campus. I demanded that they hold that debate on campus. Even though the location of the debate was changed, the only place that the debate was advertised was in the LDS Institute building, which was also in violation. That meant that the only kids who came to the debate on the main campus were the Institute kids. All the questions aimed toward me were, "Why do you hate Mormonism?"

I explained. "I don't hate Mormonism. Half of my family is Mormon, and I think Mormonism's a wonderful religion." I care about equality, but it seems that they didn't care very much. I ran two years in a row. I had kids knock my brochures out of my hand and I also had kids call me a Christ killer in college, just like they did when I was in grade school.

What would you say to kids who are suffering because of religious discrimination?

Number one is to realize that there's nothing wrong with you. There's something wrong with them. It's a wonderful opportunity to choose not to discriminate against others. Rather than needing those who are against you for friends, find friends who aren't so closed-minded. There are almost eight billion people on this planet, and if you have a really big high school, there may be two thousand students at your school. That is a very small number compared to the amount of people on earth. With the internet, you can connect with people who share your interests. You should choose the people who will be your nearest and dearest friends and won't be hateful toward you. Those who mistreat you are really being foolish.

I have no interest in talking to those who bullied me. I've forgiven them. My best friend harbored a lot of anger toward the bullies for many years, and he has recently done what it takes to start to forgive them. I, on the other hand, have looked back on all those people and all those hurtful things and I say, "Well, you've tried to hurt me, but you didn't. You've tried to be important and meaningful in my life in a negative way, and you didn't succeed." One of the things I enjoy about the Jewish Holidays is the saying "They tried to kill us; we survived." That's my take on life: they tried to oppress me, they tried to destroy me, they failed, and I overcame.

As I've gone back and seen the kids who've bullied me, it's fascinating to see that they haven't had great lives. The kids who were so popular at school weren't so great when they stepped out into the real world. After high school, no one cared how much money their mom or dad made. No one cared about the proximity of their house to the school. They had a real shift in their world because suddenly they weren't entitled to the adoration of the community. On the other hand, the kids who had always dealt with diversity were far more prepared to go out and achieve in the real world.

Those who have been bullied turned out a lot better than those who bullied them. Maybe it makes you tougher. Maybe it makes you stronger, kinder, and filled with love. That's my statement about being bullied.

***

"You're either the problem or the solution to the ills of humanity. Don't be the problem."

~Timothy Pina, *Hearts of Haiti*

Bullying Needs to Stop
by Taha

Taha was fourteen years old at the time of this writing.

***

I've been bullied for being a Muslim in America.

What country were you born in?
I was born in the U.S.

Who do you live with?
I live with my parents and my twelve-year-old sister.

Are your parents Muslim?
My dad's a Muslim and my mom sort of is. She's not practicing right now.

Can you give me a little bit of background about what Muslims believe?
Muslims believe in the five pillars of the sun.

The first pillar is Shahadah, which means the Creed, which all Muslims believe.

There's no deity to worship except one God, and Muhammad is his messenger.

The second pillar of the sun is Salah, which is Prayer. All Muslims should pray five times a day, starting from early morning before the sun rises, then at noon, afternoon, sunset, and night.

How long is a prayer?
Usually about five minutes. The prayers aren't very long.

The third pillar is Zakat, which is almsgiving. All Muslims pay two and a half percent of their annual income to the poor and needy.

The fourth pillar is Sawn, which means fasting. All Muslims should fast in the month of Ramadan, which is the Holy month. We fast one day from sunrise to sunset. Muslims use the lunar calendar and the month of Ramadan varies.

The fifth and last pillar is Hajj, which is the pilgrimage to Mecca. This pilgrimage should be made at least once in our lifetime, if we have the health or the money to make the trip.

Have you been to Mecca?
I haven't yet.

Is it hard to be a Muslim in the U.S.?
I try not to talk to people about it, you know. If someone asks me, I'll say that I'm Muslim, but otherwise I won't bring it up in a conversation. I'm afraid of being bullied and being called a terrorist, or being told that I should get out of the country. When Osama bin Laden, the al-Qaeda terrorist, was killed, everyone was saying that my father was killed.

Have things changed for Muslims after 9/11?
Yes. It's been hard for my father to find a job because of discrimination. It's hard for him to work because people also make fun of him on the job. A lot of Muslims have been losing their jobs and going back to their home country because they just can't stand the discrimination that they're facing.

What kind of job does your dad do normally?
He's a plumber, but right now he's just doing side jobs.

Has it been that way ever since 9/11?
Yeah, pretty much.

Our country also went through a recession.
Yeah, the recession made it even harder.

Where were your parents born?
My mom was born in Brazil, and my dad's from Tunisia, North Africa.

Was he trained as a plumber in this country?
Yeah. He's done all his plumbing here.

Does your mom have a job?
Yes, she takes care of older people.

What kind of bullying have you or people you know experienced because of your religion?
The usual, with people calling us terrorists, but sometimes it gets more aggressive. Some kids I know at the Mosque get taunted so much

that they start moving away from their religion and hanging out with the wrong people because they want to be cool. And then they start doing bad things.

Do they start doing drugs?
Yeah. It doesn't go too far, but we don't see them as often as we used to.

It's hard to stick up for yourself when you have that much trouble.
Exactly.

Has it affected you like that?
At one point, I just wanted to stop practicing my religion. But now I'm holding on and getting through it. I found that my religion is more important to me than what other people think.

Do people ever throw things at your house or write negative messages to your family?
No.

When you go out, do you ever fear for your safety?
I might have some fear, but not too much.

Do your neighbors treat your family well?
We don't really talk to our neighbors very much.

Do you just kind of stay to yourselves?
Yeah.

Even though people bully you, have you always had friends?
Yeah, I have friends. I've always had good friends who've stayed with me and helped me, even when I was being bullied.

Good! What would you like to tell other kids who are being bullied because of their religion?
Kids should always stay focused on their religion. Your religion is more important than what other people think. In the end, it's God who judges.
I'd also like to say that not all Muslims are bad, even though some Muslims are bad, just like there are bad people in any other religions. Muslims in America felt bad when 9/11 happened, just like everyone else.
Thanks for getting out the message that bullying needs to stop and

that bullying anyone for any reason is just wrong.

***

"I don't like bullies. No one has the right to take or hurt just because they can."

~Pittacus Lore, *Rise of Nine*

Bullied by Religion
by Victoria Reynolds

Victoria is the author of Transcending Fear: 7 Steps to Rise Above Fear and Fall in Love with Life; www.victoriareynolds.com

***

I was born into a closed religious, polygamist community where I never really fit in.

Because I was different I was bullied both by my peers and by their parents. As a teenager, I convinced my parents to allow me to attend public high school. In public school, the bullying escalated to swearing profanities at me, eventually leading to physical violence and rape.

My book *Fly, Fly Away*, soon to be released, is focused on religious bullying and the bullying that occurred in the public school system as a result of my parents' chosen lifestyle. I left as a teenager when I could no longer endure the pain from both systems. My book *Transcending Fear* is my mid-life discovery that those beliefs from my childhood religion were still pushing me around as an adult in a very subtle and subconscious way, and how I finally, once and for all, cleared those beliefs from my mind, heart, body, and soul.

Where were you born, and what was the prevalent religion?
I was born into a closed religious community in Montana. The entire community practiced Fundamentalist Mormonism, which is based on the religion that Mormons practiced in the 1800s. While many of the beliefs remain the same as mainstream Mormons, we also practiced polygamy in my community, which was abandoned by the Mormon Church in the nineteenth century.

Tell me about your household. Did you have two parents, or did your father have more than one wife?
We did have a large family, but I only had one mother until I was in high school. Most of the men in the community had at least three wives, and many of them shared their homes. It was believed in our religion that three wives were necessary in order for men and women to ascend to the highest levels of heaven after death. This belief had my parents in a constant state of worry. Since no other women were joining our family, they thought they had done something wrong and that God did not

believe they were worthy of polygamy.

My family wasn't openly bullied by the church leaders, but we were well aware that we were second-class citizens with a second-class name. There's a royal hierarchy in my parents' religion, and we were at the bottom.

Why do you say you were second-class citizens? And why was your family at the bottom?

Those few families who left mainstream Mormonism in the 1800s and began their own religious movement were treated like royalty. It was believed that their descendants would have a "go straight to the highest level of heaven" card just because of their last name. They intermarried between each other and only added other families with non-royal last names because of the additional wives they needed.

I knew from the time I was a little girl that I belonged to a second-class family and I would never earn the position of first wife to any man who could ensure my place in heaven. The church taught that women couldn't get to heaven without being married to the right man. Men like my father had to work extra hard to prove their worthiness in heaven, as well as his worthiness to live the law of plural marriage.

During the time of my own personal crisis, my father was coerced by community leaders to find another wife or be expelled from the community. My father's new wife, who I refused to call Mother, moved into the basement of our house while my mother and most of her children remained in the upstairs portion.

What kind of private school did you attend?

I attended the only school in our community. It was a religion-based school that only taught academics which were supported by my religion. We weren't taught science or world history, and very little American history. There was certainly no sex education or biology.

Was this a very large school? Did you have several grades, or were all the children together in one classroom?

The school my older siblings attended was a one-room log cabin. By the time I was six years old and ready for school, a new building had been built that housed the school, along with all church and community-related programs. Our building had six classrooms, a large gathering room, a kitchen, and a baptismal font.

What kind of bullying did you experience from your peers and their parents?

The religion itself was the bully. A parent's acceptance in heaven was determined by how well they kept their children in the religion. Therefore, parents were encouraged to bring their children into salvation by whatever means necessary. As a result, I was frequently spanked for asking questions or for what was seen as inappropriate behavior, like not crossing my arms or talking during church.

I was bullied by boys, even at a very young age, because I was a girl and they were taught that girls had no real worth. I was bullied by the other children in my community because I didn't want to follow the rules and be who the religion expected me to be. I was also bullied by their parents, being told I was a bad influence on their children.

Did your parents know this kind of bullying went on at school?

I had been taught as a child not to defend or express myself. The children in my community only acted out in the way they saw their parents act out, parroting their parents' beliefs and comments. This is the way small children act when they haven't learned the value and importance of their own voice. The bullying in my elementary school was never dealt with by any adult because bullying was not a term recognized by our system.

What rules did you break, and why did the parents think you were a bad influence?

As a child, I was ostracized by everyone except one girl who became my best friend all through elementary school. We were inseparable except for a period of time when I had a non-communicable skin disorder that everyone in the community treated like a plague. It was believed that I had this disorder because Satan had brought it upon me for my actions. I lived in fear because I didn't know what I could have done wrong except the belief deep inside me that my religion was not right, even as much as I wanted it to be. Maybe I didn't fold my arms tight enough in Sunday school or stay quiet enough in religion class. Could I have laughed too loudly on the school playground? Maybe it was my desire to wear pants, climb trees, and play with boys instead of wearing dresses and sitting at home with dolls and a sewing machine.

When I was in the eighth grade a male teacher made open advances toward me that became continually bolder throughout the year. One afternoon I finally had enough of him when, in front of the classroom, he put his arms around me and pulled me close to his body. In an environment where even my parents and family members did not hug me, this was entirely too much for me to tolerate. My rebellious streak became obvious after I told my teacher, who was also the unquestioned priesthood leader, to take his hands off me. I was expelled from school and told never to return. After that day, I was no longer allowed to associate with any of the children in the community, as if my independent streak would rub off onto the other kids as contagiously as the skin disorder I once had.

Were your parents or your church leaders preparing you to marry at a young age?

When I was eleven years old, I was promised in marriage to a friend of my father's. This was a man I despised, and I was sickened and devastated when I overheard the conversation between the two men. It felt as though I was nothing more than a slave used for bartering between my current owner and the man who would eventually own me. Although the leadership of my religion changed hands and arranged marriages went by the wayside, my father often brought up the name of his friend with hope in his eyes that I would recognize my destiny.

Will you tell about the experiences you had in public high school?

Our private school ended with eighth grade, and girls were discouraged from continuing their education. It was believed that girls didn't need an education because they weren't expected to work outside the home except to volunteer as an elementary school teacher or religion teacher. I wanted more education and wanted to be more than a menial housewife. I'd heard of women who worked outside the home and wanted to be one of them. I convinced my parents to let me go to public high school, completely unaware of what I had put myself into.

Were the kids in the public high school also from the Fundamentalist Mormon group, or were they kids from other religions? Were there other girls from your church in the high school, or only boys?

There were a few other students from my religion in the public high school. I was the first girl who didn't have the "right" last name to attend public school. And, since I had already been ostracized by others from my community, I was on my own as I attempted to navigate through a world I knew nothing about. I knew nothing of science, history, boys, or my own biology. I had been told by my parents that my husband would eventually tell me how my body worked and where babies came from. In high school, I was teased, called very hurtful names in the hallways, beaten up in the bathroom, and eventually raped.

Did the girls beat you up?

Yes. I was bullied after a boy in school claimed to have sex with me and eventually other boys in school joined the game of who had the best sex with me. I had no idea what sex was—only that it was bad and that I didn't do it. The girls were threatened by the belief that I was having sex with their boyfriends or with boys they wanted for boyfriends. I had always been nice to the boys in school, and my niceness and naiveté were seen by other students as flirtation. My innocence was my downfall.

It began with name-calling in the hallway, followed by being shoved up against the lockers between classes. Then the girls started following me into the bathroom where they threatened me. One time I was restrained while they pushed my head into a toilet. It progressed into a gang attack on me in the locker room after school, when four girls hit and kicked me until the school janitor knocked on the door and scared them away.

When you were going through all of this hate and bullying, did you have any friends who stood by you? Did you have a boyfriend?

My one friend all throughout elementary school could not associate with me anymore. In high school, I was completely alone. My freshman year I befriended another girl who didn't know anyone, but once the rumors started, she abandoned me as well. I had a fantasy boyfriend who I knew would never even give me the time of day because he was royalty, but pretending he could someday like me gave me something to look forward to.

Were you raped by a boy from your religion?

No. I had been invited by a few girls we called "gentiles" to attend a keg party, which was an annual tradition for the kids in my high school. I had never tasted beer and had no idea what to expect. After drinking, a few boys invited me to be alone with them and I thought nothing of it. As I lay on the ground drunk with the world spinning around me, one of the boys raped me. I thought to myself, "This must be how babies are made." It was almost as though I was detached from my body. Under the pretense of rescuing me, another boy invited me into his truck and forced me to perform oral sex on him.

Did you ever tell a teacher or talk to the principal about the bullying? Was there any kind of help from the administration at your school?

I attempted to tell the principal, who, instead of assisting me, insisted I did something to bring on the actions of the other kids. All of it was blamed on me and nothing was ever done to discipline the other students, except the boy who had started it all. His pre-existing juvenile record only brought him more attention. After the rape, when life became too painful for me to bear, I dropped out of high school.

How did you get away from the Fundamentalist community? What did you take with you? Where did you go and how did you survive? We hear about people who will take in girls from polygamist communities and help them get on their feet.

When I ran away from home at the age of seventeen, it wasn't due to the impending marriage my father had arranged. I was afraid that I would never find true love and instead live in a loveless marriage, as I saw in so many of the marriages in the community we called The Ranch. The choice was either to commit suicide or take my chances alone in the world.

Not long after I made the decision not to take my own life, I was called by a friend of mine who had left a few months earlier. A family in Utah with two teenage daughters had agreed to take my friend into their home until she was ready to survive on her own. She told me that the family she was staying with had agreed to take me as well, and that all I needed to do was find a ride to Salt Lake City. Not long after that, the opportunity arose when a funeral in my community brought relatives from Utah. I convinced one of the teenage boys that my parents had given me permission to leave. I packed a brown paper bag with my teddy bear, my toothbrush, a pair of pajamas, and a few changes of clothing. I climbed into the backseat of the boy's car, along with a few people I didn't know, and drove away.

I stayed with the family for a few months until I found a job and an apartment, and then I was on my own. There were no organizations at that time to assist with my adjustment, no support system, no therapy programs, and no examples to follow. Terrified of being ostracized and tormented in the mainstream Mormon community of Salt Lake City, I told no one where I came from or what I had been through. I forged my way through the world, attempting to fit in as I made up a story about where I came from and who I was. For all intents and purposes I was Mormon, just like everyone else, but deep inside I knew it wasn't right for me. The fear of leaving the only background I'd ever known prevented me from finding my own truth for a very long time.

Is your family still living in the community where you grew up?

My parents have both passed away, but they both lived in the community until they died. My oldest sister and her family still live there. She's still married to the man my father gave her to. She's the second of his three wives. Most of her children still live in the community, and I suspect will eventually follow the polygamist lifestyle. It's very difficult not to succumb to the beliefs of those around us and the beliefs that we are raised with as children. I talk to my sister occasionally. She's a very sweet woman who lives a very simple, yet complicated, life. We have nothing in common other than a set of parents and a history in a secluded secretive lifestyle. My other siblings have all left polygamy. Many of them were eventually baptized into the Mormon Church. My connection and communication with them is limited to the occasional Facebook post.

What would you like to say about bullying?
I now see the religion as the bully. I understand bullies and see them for who they really are. Bullies are who they are because of their own pain. The kids who bullied me in high school were from broken homes with abusive parents, and they took their pain out on me as an easy target.

***

"Everyone has problems which are usually results of their environment. The key to greatness is to have the ability to rise above all of it and contributing one's energy to help better our world"
~ Timothy Pina, *Hearts for Haiti*

We Don't Practice Religion
by Victoria Reynolds

I have witnessed religious bullying at my children's public elementary school. Not because of religious preference, but because we choose not to include any established religion in their lives. The bullying comes from Christian kids who tell other kids they are going to hell because they don't go to church. That's not very Christ-like!

You say your kids are bullied because they don't practice religion. Will you tell about the kinds of experiences they have had?

My children are in elementary school. They have been told by other children that they are going to hell because they don't go to church. My daughter has been called a "cheesehead" because she doesn't believe God is a man. "Cheesehead" might not seem like much, but it's a word that doesn't get the kids in trouble at school. Essentially, it is a word that is used to insinuate that she is a total loser. I know the teachings of Christ better than many Christians, and what Christ taught was love. What these children are doing is the opposite of what Christ taught, which saddens me deeply. My kids do enjoy school for the most part, and have many friends. I teach my children about the importance of open-mindedness and acceptance of others' beliefs. I have mentioned this issue to the principal and school counselor, both of whom take this matter very seriously. My children are not the only ones who have been affected by this; I have spoken to other non-religious parents whose children have experienced the same taunting as mine. First graders telling other first graders that they are going to hell is completely unacceptable and not something I am willing to have my children tolerate. Tolerating it in first grade invites it to escalate over the years until the ruthlessness of high school takes root and years of self-esteem building becomes necessary.

Have they had to change schools?

I'm fortunate to send my children to one of the best public schools in California. My kids will stay there as we work through the issues that come with life. The staff is very loving, supportive, and proactive. Fortunately, most of the parents and children at the school are genuinely kind people. There are a few students who don't understand that religious bullying is just as hurtful as any other form of bullying.

I teach my children how to stand up for themselves in compassion and understanding for those who attempt to bully them. I teach my children self-respect, self-honor, self-compassion, self-forgiveness, and self-love. Only when we hold those for ourselves can we truly see others through the eye of understanding and without judgment of who we think they need to be. We are all doing the best we can to make our way through this journey of life on this crazy planet we call home. We are all searching for the same thing: our own inner sense of happiness.

***

"The common mistake that bullies make is assuming that because someone is nice that he or she is weak. In fact, it takes considerable strength and character to be a good person."

~Mary Elizabeth Williams

Tattooed On My Memory
by Paulette Inman

Paulette "Pendragon" Inman is the author of the Shinehah Saga series of five books for YA readers; www.shinehahsaga.com

***

I grew up as a Mormon in a predominantly Catholic high school in Phoenix, Arizona. There were only thirteen members of the LDS (Mormon) Church in my high school when I attended. We knew each other very well and formed lasting friendships through our off-campus seminary class.

In my younger years of school, I didn't stand out as much because of my religion. When I got to high school, the other kids began to treat me differently because of my beliefs and standards.

I was teased a lot in school. However, not all of those times were because of my religion. The kids had plenty of other things to taunt me about, like my name or my non-Barbie looks. The girls especially enjoyed pointing out my non-stylish clothing. Like many LDS kids, I came from a large family and we shopped at thrift stores and carried on the tradition of handing down clothes from kid to kid. I was the fifth of six kids, so by the time the clothes were passed on to me, they were far from the latest fashion. Imagine a girl in the late nineties with handmade shorts down past her knees and T-shirts that only boys typically wore. I didn't see my clothes as ugly. I dressed modestly, as counseled in my church classes, and so I tried my best to ignore the other girls.

Looking back, perhaps the kids weren't picking on me for the fact that I was a Mormon necessarily—I'm not sure they even knew about the church specifically. Rather, they picked on me because of the way I lived. Things like not drinking, not smoking, not doing drugs, dressing modestly, and being a virgin were targeted. Most of the taunting didn't bother me because it was over beliefs that I had adopted as my own, and not just from my religious viewpoint. What hurt, however, was when I lost close friends because of those beliefs. It happened twice, involving four friends, and those moments are tattooed on my memory.

I had been best friends with a girl since we were in kindergarten together, and as far as I was concerned, we were still best friends. We were in our freshman math class, both standing at the chalkboard as we worked out a particularly long algebraic equation. I was nose deep in my calculations when she tapped me on the shoulder.

"We can't be friends anymore," she said out of nowhere. I thought it was a joke, but she didn't laugh. I noticed a few other kids watching us as if they had urged her to get it over with. "I have new friends now," she said, "and they won't let me hang out with them if we're still friends, so we can't hang out anymore. You understand, right?"

No, I didn't understand. At all. And I told her so.

"We've been friends for a long time," she explained, "but I was innocent back then. I'm changing. You wouldn't do the stuff my new friends want to do. You're Mormon," she added in a whisper. "I'm sorry."

Tears filled my eyes, but I remember telling her in a hushed voice, "If they're doing things that I wouldn't do, perhaps you shouldn't be doing them, either." It didn't sway her. True to her word, we never hung out again. It wasn't until years after I graduated that I received a letter from her expressing how she wanted to change her life for the better, and every time she thought of it, she thought of me.

The second time I lost friends because of my religion was shortly after I graduated from high school. My "gang," as we called it, four other friends and I who hung out all the time and usually played video games, included an LDS boy named James. Like my old friend from kindergarten, I had known James all my life. Our families were good friends and in the same church congregation together. With both James and me, the gang never indulged inappropriate activities. They never pressured us to go drinking or ventured into immoral pairings. Maybe it's because James was such a big guy that they didn't want to bully him into things they knew he wouldn't even humor. Either way, he became a rock that I knew wouldn't break under pressure and our friends seemed to respect him for it.

After we graduated from high school, James turned nineteen and left on a two-year mission to Argentina. Without him, the entire dynamic of the group changed. Within two months, the other three friends decided that having me as part of the group was holding them back. They wanted to drink and have porn parties. They told me bluntly that if I was there, it made them feel guilty. So I was ditched.

I wish I could say this had no lasting effect on me, but I struggled with trusting other people for many years. I preferred to engage in activities that only relied on me for success, such as writing, music, sign language, and martial arts.

I wrote to James while he served in Argentina, and he inspired me to prepare for a mission as well. I began saving money while I attended college. Most of the religious discrimination ended with high school. College students seemed too busy and concerned with their education to worry about the differences between their fellow students. Value was based on your own educational dedication in class. I didn't see or feel any religious taunting again until after I left college and started submitting the paperwork for my mission.

Of all places to feel bullied again, I didn't expect it in a professional medical office. Part of the requirements to serve a mission at the time was to be current on shots and have a complete medical exam, including a chest X-ray. I arrived in the medical office for my X-ray and filled out their patients' form. One of the questions was why the X-ray was needed. I wrote that it was part of my missionary healthcare requirements, gave the papers back to the nurse, and sat down, waiting for my turn. Soon, I heard the two nurses at the front desk reviewing my file.

"For a mission?" one asked.

The other chuckled and in a mocking voice, replied, "God told me to get a chest X-ray."

They both laughed as they entered my information into the computer, making a few other comments. I don't know if they realized that I, along with everyone in the waiting area, heard them. I didn't say anything, and perhaps I should have. But regardless of their personal religious outlooks, what they did was inappropriate. I remember wondering if I should have written something else down on that line — anything else that wouldn't have merited their taunting — but I didn't see the need to hide the fact that I wanted to serve a mission.

When they called me back for the X-ray, the nurse who helped me — she wasn't either of the two at the desk — glanced over my record and asked, "This is for a religious mission?" I could hear the confusion in her voice.

I straightened my back and replied, "Yes. I am volunteering to serve a mission for The Church of Jesus Christ of Latter-day Saints, and they need to know if I have any health problems that would keep me from serving in any given country of the world for the next eighteen months of my life."

She smiled, congratulated me on my valor, and asked if I knew where I would be going. I didn't, but the moment taught me that it didn't matter if others teased me for my beliefs and aspirations. They tease because they don't understand.

I served a wonderful mission in Sydney, Australia, where I faced a fair share of religious discrimination consistently. We were yelled at, had doors slammed on us, dogs sent to chase us, and even an egg thrown our way, but none of it changed who I was. When they realized that we lived what we believed, confusion turned to respect, and religious differences no longer mattered.

When I got home, everything came full circle. I hooked up with the one man I respected through all those years: James. We've been married for almost twelve years now and have two beautiful sons. Nobody teases us for having a strong, united marriage, even if it is built on our mutual religious standards. I hope through us that our children will learn not only to withstand those who bully them, but perhaps even teach the bullies how wonderful life can be.

Section Seven

Learn From the Experts

"No one should ever be bullied, and all children and adults need to band together to put a stop to it."

~Gabriela Castillo

Kid Power: Knowing How to be in Charge
by Irene van der Zande

Irene van der Zande is the author of Bullying—What Adults Need to Know to Keep Kids Safe, Face Bullying With Confidence: Creating Cultures of Respect and Safety for All Ages and Stages of Life, and many other books and articles.

***

I am the director and founder of a nonprofit organization called Kidpower Teenpower Fullpower International. You can visit www.kidpower.org to learn about our empowering and effective workshops and educational resources.

The inspiration for starting Kidpower happened in 1985 when a man in a public place in the middle of the day threatened to kidnap a group of young children, including my own two. I stopped him by yelling at him and calling to a bystander for help. At that point, my career was as a community organizer, helping many local nonprofit organizations with management, program development, and funding. I had just finished writing my first book, *1, 2, 3 The Toddler Years*, and had anticipated writing the next book in the series when we had this frightening experience. My plans changed and I got together with martial artists, law enforcement officers, educators, and health professionals. We could not find any existing programs that focused on how to be safe with people that were fun, effective, empowering, and safe, so decided to create our own services. Our goal was to provide services that gave practical skills on how to protect children, teens, and adults, including those with special needs, from any kind of emotional or physical violence, including bullying, teasing, harassment, and abuse.

We established Kidpower as a nonprofit in 1989 and have now served over three million people worldwide through our workshops and educational resources. We have books and articles about child protection, positive communication, and personal safety for all ages and abilities, from before birth through old age.

Have you ever been bullied?

When I was in the second grade, a long time ago, there was a group of girls led by one girl who shunned me, leaving me out of every game and every activity. Recess after recess, lunchtime after lunchtime, I sat outside on the sidewalk by the locked classroom door and read while waiting for playtime to be over. I can't remember there being adults around, and it never occurred to me to tell my parents or ask anyone for help. This went on until the fifth grade, when these girls cornered me in the bathroom and started to push and shove me. I kicked the ringleader in the shins and she started crying. All these girls went to complain to the teacher. I never thought she knew what was going on because she had never approached me. To my great astonishment, she believed me instead of them. After that, the bullying finally stopped. I also experienced harassment and those types of things that you don't question when you're a child. But as an adult, I look back and say, "I wish I had had Kidpower when I was growing up. It sure would have helped."

Kidpower Makes Life Easier

Adults learn how to advocate for creating cultures of positive peer relationships at school and everywhere, how to intervene powerfully and respectfully in the moment when kids are acting unsafely, and how to teach kids skills for taking charge of their own emotional and physical safety. Kids learn how to protect their feelings, to project an attitude of confidence, to walk away from trouble, to set boundaries, to act safely and respectfully towards others no matter how they feel inside, and to be really persistent in getting adult help when they need it.

Kidpower provides an extensive free online library, including articles, videos, and podcasts. We also have a newsletter and a bullying solutions resource page. We are leading the establishment of September as International Child Protection Month, which will inspire, support, and honor the importance of adult leadership in keeping young people safe from bullying, abuse, and other dangers, and in advocating for their well-being.

Kidpower provides coaching and support to families dealing with bullying, as well as training for their kids. Often, a variety of actions are needed: advocating with school authorities, helping the child or teen find new positive peer groups, changing schools if necessary, staying very connected emotionally with this young person and stating repeatedly that the bullying is not her or his fault, and sometimes getting professional counseling. One girl, who I'll call Cindy, was horribly cyber-bullied by a group of girls, who made a page called "I hate Cindy" on Facebook. It was devastating because a couple hundred kids said that they liked the page. As an adult, I would have a hard time if a couple hundred of my peers said they liked it that someone said they hated me. During our Teenpower class, Cindy was able to practice skills on how to protect herself that were a great help, and we provided coaching to her parents on how to provide support to their daughter.

Another student had been repeatedly brutally beaten up by some kids until he ended up in the hospital. His mom said that after our Kidpower class, he was able to stop seventeen incidents without ever having to get violent because he had more confidence and he could anticipate trouble. He started acting like he was in charge of himself, and other kids stopped bothering him.

We also work with kids who bully. One mother brought in her twelve-year-old son, saying, "I want him to make it through high school. I don't want him to get kicked out because he keeps getting in fights." It turned out that he would get into fights because kids teased him. Through Kidpower, he learned to be in charge of the things he said and did and not to take in hurtful words from others.

If kids are really upset inside, we teach them how to get centered and how to stay calm. We help them look at the safest choices. Rather than thinking, "I need to fight to protect myself from an insult," they will learn that, "I can protect myself from an insult without fighting. I can protect myself from the inside."

Our practice is pretty realistic. Instructors role play, gently shoving a student and saying something in a mocking voice, like, "Hey, kid." We coach our students in how to leave calmly, without escalating the situation. We teach them to leave with awareness, not acting like a victim. After a practice, one boy said, "I just learned that it takes more courage not to fight than to fight."

Our books, including *Bullying: What Adults Need to Know and Do to Keep Kids Safe,* have many success stories showing how practicing a few skills prepared kids to stay calm and make safer choices rather than being overwhelmed.

We have centers in thirty states and countries where our instructors organize and teach workshops. In addition, the knowledge and skills Kidpower teaches are available everywhere through our online library and affordable publications. The Kidpower 30-Skill Challenge is on our website and is used by educators, youth group leaders, and parents to introduce and practice skills. Our low-cost Safety Comics include social stories using safety skills in an entertaining way and give readers directions on how to practice skills that kids even teach to each other.

We call what we teach People Safety, which means being emotionally and physically safe with people, including yourself. When your body is healthy, you can resist all kinds of diseases and have more fun doing things with your body. In the same manner, if you have strong People Safety skills, you can prevent most problems and have more fun with people.

There are things parents didn't know when they were growing up or while raising their kids, like not putting grease on a sunburn or using a seatbelt, but now we know differently. Knowing how to be in charge can help prevent bullying. Most people say, "Why didn't I know about Kidpower before? This should be in all our schools!" The more people who know about Kidpower, the more people we can help.

Our video, Walk in Another's Shoes, was created by teens for teens to raise awareness about bullying. Our One Million Safer Kids video shows young people having fun practicing skills that can help stop bullying and other kinds of emotional and physical violence. Our newest book, *Face Bullying With Confidence: Creating Cultures of Respect and Safety for All Ages and Stages of Life*, was inspired by the many adults who told me that they were using People Safety skills to stop bullying behavior at their workplaces, social groups, places of worship, homes, and senior centers.

Here is the link for our Bullying Prevention Resource page: http://www.kidpower.org/bullying

***

"If you turn and face the other way when someone is being bullied, you might as well be the bully too.

~Unknown

Kids are the Real Experts on School Climate
by William Preble

William Preble, Ed.D. , is the author of: Transforming School Climate and co-author Learning: Beyond Bullying and Compliance by William Preble and Rick Gordon, and The Respectful School: How Educators and Students Can Conquer Hate and Harassment by Stephen Wessler and William Preble

***

National School Climate Standards: The school has:
1. A vision about what it means to be a safe, respectful, effective school. And school climate data is collected to assess how well the school is achieving its vision.
2. Policies and systems aimed at student support including: clear norms of accepted student and adult behavior, student behavioral support systems (rather than zero-tolerance disciplinary systems), anti-bullying and harassment policies and procedures, and advisory systems to build adult-student and peer-to-peer relationships.
3. Respectful effective teaching practices which include: personalized and inclusionary learning processes that respect and support individual student learning differences, that emphasize student growth, student engagement, and building on students' talents and strengths.
4. A safe, respectful, and welcoming school environment for students, parents, community, and teachers.
5. A focus on student empowerment, civic engagement, and active student participation in the school and community, as well as an emphasis on the fair, respectful and equal treatment of all students.

What is School Climate?
My colleague Jerome Freiberg says, "School climate is like the air we breathe; no one notices it until it becomes toxic." There are many things that affect school climate, including student safety and relationships with peers and teachers, bullying and harassment, teacher morale, the leadership style of the principal, the school's approach to discipline, and

the extent to which students are engaged in learning.

Kids Are the Real Experts of School Climate

One student told me he thought "The real school climate is what happens in a school when the grownups aren't around." If this is true, then educators need to work closely with students, and listen to them if they want to really understand what is happening in their schools. The bonus that comes from recognizing that students can offer important information and expertise when it comes to understanding school climate is that not only will you get more "valid" information when you "ask the kids," but treating students as experts on school climate, rather than as the problem, will improve school climate.

School climate is all about perception. The same school can be harsh, dangerous, and toxic for some students, while at the same time, it can be welcoming, safe, and respectful for other students. If you really want to understand school climate you need to talk to kids, lots of different kinds of kids.

The Center for School Climate in Learning works with students, teachers, and administrators to collect data that helps schools understand students' and teachers' perceptions of the school. We then work with diverse teams of students and their teachers and principals to use this information to help schools begin an honest, open discussion on school climate. This process helps school leaders better understand their schools and find new ways to build respect and improve school climate, student engagement, and learning.

A lot of schools try to tackle the issue of bullying in isolation, without connecting it to the larger issue of school climate. We like to work with student "experts" to show grownups how school climate is related to bullying, as well as to the school's approach to discipline, student and teacher roles in the school, and how school climate goes much further than kids being unkind to each other by bullying.

Defining Bullying, Harassment, and Drama

We have found that unkind behavior, bullying, and racial and sexual harassment can be problems in any school, no matter how much the adults might think their school is "just fine." The problem comes when schools confuse the different forms of disrespectful behavior and call them all bullying.

When you involve students in discussions and collect data from all students, you begin to see the problems much more clearly. There are nearly always individual students or groups of students in a school who have less power or lower social status than other student groups. These can be poor kids, gay and lesbian kids—or those who are thought to be gay—non-athletes, kids who are overweight, students who struggle with learning, students of color, or students from different cultures or religions. Bullying and harassment in schools is all about powerful students, whether an individual bully or groups of students, using their power in hurtful and abusive ways toward students with less power. Schools that successfully deal with bullying behavior understand these power differences and how they play out inside the school—and online during and after school hours.

Over the past few years, many states have recognized bullying as a problem. This is because of a set of high profile teen suicides thought to be caused by bullying, as well as because bullying is increasingly viewed as being a catalyst in many school shooting incidents. So states have passed important new laws, and new school policies have been put in place that have resulted in schools taking bullying much more seriously.

It's important for kids to know whether or not their state has an anti-bullying law and if there are school policies in place that are designed to protect them from bullying. If there is a law in place, it tells students and parents what steps they should take if they have a complaint, and how to deal with bullying effectively. If kids know the laws, they will know what to do, especially if adults in their schools are saying, "Don't worry, bullying is part of growing up" or "We don't see bullying as a problem in our school."

These days, it seems like *everything* is considered bullying. We hear about bullying all the time. The news is saturated with awful, and often confusing, bullying stories. It becomes a huge problem when everything is called bullying because everyone gets confused about what bullying *really* is, and they don't recognize that sometimes it's not bullying at all, but a problem of discrimination.

We help schools to understand what is and is not considered bullying. We also help them to understand the state and school bullying policies. Sometimes the problems should not be dealt with as bullying, but as harassment. This includes sexual harassment, racial harassment, and discrimination against kids with disabilities. When a school classifies these infringements as bullying, it's a step backward. Harassment is illegal under the civil rights law, and is a serious offence. The consequences for bullying are much less severe than the consequences for violating somebody's civil rights. Part of the challenge for school leaders and students is to learn to see how bullying and harassment differ.

The next thing I think is really important is helping schools understand the difference between bullying and the day-to-day conflict—we call this drama—that happens so frequently in schools.

After defining the difference between drama and bullying, we ask kids if there's any drama in the school, and they almost always say, "There's tons of drama in this school."

School leaders and students need to understand that the difference between drama and bullying is primarily a difference of power relations between the students. It is drama when the participants are not separated by differences in their social, academic, economic, political, and power status; just plain old social conflict. If a school uses the anti-bullying policies to deal with routine conflicts, they will have overreacted. Their overreaction can cause problems, because it is not fair or appropriate to categorize social conflict or drama between students as bullying, when there is no abuse due to power differences between the students.

Bullying is always an imbalance between kids in terms of their social power or their physical power.

When you talk about a child being bullied, I think it's very important to look into that and decide if s/he's involved in social conflict with peers or if it's really bullying. If it's bullying, you need to be able to point to an imbalance in power. For example, if a group of kids is picking on a child, that's a clear imbalance of power because there are many against one. Or if the child has some sort of learning disability and the kids are regular ed kids who have more social power, that certainly is bullying. Really getting at the difference between conflict and bullying involves identification of the power deferential invested there. *Is the person using power to hurt somebody else?* That really cuts to the chase. That's the kind of work we do, and it's not easy; it's really kind of technical. But the alternative is that everything becomes bullying, and that doesn't help anyone.

What do you do if somebody has been singled out because of their race? How would you handle that differently?

I would look at the school's racial discrimination and harassment policies, which every school is required to have. I would draw the attention of the principal to the incident of racial harassment and tell them to deal with it immediately and seriously or they could potentially be ignoring the child's civil rights. Some school districts get sued because, rather than addressing the problem of harassment, they give the kids who are bullying detention or keep them in for recess, and never get to the issue of racial harassment. You need to point to civil rights laws or point to the policies against racial harassment in schools and deal with it as harassment. I would be very careful not to call that bullying.

What are some of the other categories that fall into the catch-all term of bullying?

Sexual harassment is one problem that doesn't always get the attention it should. A lot of the gender-based persecution they call bullying is much more serious than that. Then there is also the whole issue of calling kids "retard." Kids with lesser physical or cognitive disabilities are protected under harassment laws.

Being different is one of the most common reasons that students are bullied or harassed in a school. This is something we've been struggling with as a country for a long time. We've made slow, steady progress over the last forty or fifty years to recognize that just because a kid is different, it doesn't give you the right to pick on that kid, call him a name, or socially isolate him or her.

I feel like schools need to do a better job identifying and addressing harassment. To water it all down and call it bullying is incorrect. People have fought for years to get these civil rights laws in place, and we cannot afford to ignore them or confuse them as we attempt to combat bullying.

What would be the consequences for both of those?

The state anti-bullying laws have spelled out the process that needs to be followed. In some states, such as Tennessee, there is a student handbook which spells out consequences. Consequences usually go through an escalation process. Those for a first offense often focus on understanding why the behavior was hurtful, accepting responsibility, and, in some cases, "restoring balance to the community" by working to make the person who was victimized whole again in some way. The second offense often carries a more severe consequence, and a third offense could result in a much more serious one, which could include removal from the school setting if a student is unable or unwilling to stop hurting others.

A lot of schools use a one strike and you're out zero tolerance process. This is not effective. It's really important to look at the good policies and behavioral management systems out there, such as Restorative Justice practices, Applied Behavioral Analysis processes, and peer mediation. These approaches can help give principals, teachers, and students a clear set of alternatives to punishment alone, and offer guidelines for improving behavior management.

Improve School Climate to Improve Student Learning

The most important thing that I hope schools consider is this: you can't learn when your pants are on fire. All the latest brain-based research shows us that when students are upset, afraid, or hopelessly bored, they do not learn well. School climate is also directly connected to student learning.

If we are serious about improving student learning, then we must start by working directly with and listening more closely to what our students—especially those who are somehow different and possibly less powerful—have to say about school climate, because these students are the real experts on bullying, drama, and harassment in any school.

***

"The most common way people give up their power is by thinking they don't have any."

~Alice Walker

You Can't Talk to me Like That!
Bullies to Buddies
by Izzy Kalman

Izzy Kalman, MS, Nationally Certified School Psychologist, Director of Bullies to Buddies, Inc., and author of Bullies to Buddies: How to Turn Your Enemies into Friends. His website, www.Bullies2Buddies.com, has a great deal of free, useful information for dealing with bullying by applying the Golden Rule. "There are two seminars that I frequently present to mental health professionals, teaching them to use my methods for helping clients. One is called Bully-Proofing Made Easy, which is geared to social problems of kids in school. The other is Anger Control Made Easy, which teaches how to help people with interpersonal problems throughout the lifetime. "

Author's Note: During our interview, Izzy did a role play with me to demonstrate how someone might solve a problem similar to another story in this book.

***

Izzy's Story
Izzy: I'm a psychotherapist and a school psychologist. I began working in schools in 1978, about 3 1/2 decades ago.

Many years ago a kid asked me, "What should you do if kids call you names?" For me, it was a no-brainer. I understood the sticks-and-stones slogan. I also knew that the reason anybody gets picked on over and over again is because they're getting upset by it. I asked the boy to insult me and I kept saying, "You can't talk to me like that." He had a great time as he kept on insulting me. Then I asked him to do it again, and the second time, I just let him insult me and I didn't try to stop him. He got bored and left me alone. After that incident, whenever kids would tell me they were being picked on, I would role play with them. I would have them insult me two times. The first time I would get upset, but the second time I'd stay calm and just let them insult me. I would show them how easy it was to get the insults to stop. I would ask kids to try this method for a week and see what happened. Most kids would say that it worked and the other kids had stopped picking on them.

As time went by, I made my whole routine more elaborate, adding questions and explanations that help kids understand why they're being picked on and how to make it stop. There are kids who suffer like this in every classroom and they can be taught very quickly how to solve the problem.

Over the years, I've also developed a series of rules that teach kids how to turn anyone who's being mean to them into a friend. The people we call bullies aren't only bullies. They'll support their friends. So as you use these rules, they'll respect you more and like you better. I teach that the way to get people to be nice to you is to treat them like friends.

I can even demonstrate it with you here. Let's say my mother is a garbage truck driver and you're picking on me because of my mother's occupation."

Me: I heard that your mom drives a garbage truck. I think you smell like garbage.

Izzy: Don't talk to me like that! There's nothing wrong with driving a garbage truck. And that doesn't make me smell like garbage.

Me: She drives a garbage truck and she's a dumpster diver and you know it.

Izzy: No, she's not. She empties dumpsters into the truck. She doesn't dive into the dumpsters.

Me: You're a dumpster diver just like your mother.

Izzy: I'm not a dumpster diver, and neither is my mother.

Me: You both are.

Izzy: No we're not. We don't dive into dumpsters.

Me: You look just like your mother and you smell just like your mother.

Izzy: I might look like my mother, but we don't smell.

Me: Yes, you do.

Izzy: No, we don't. You'd better stop saying that. I'm going to tell the teacher on you.

Me: Go ahead and tell the teacher, because it's the truth.

Izzy: No, it's not the truth. You can't talk about me and my mother like that and get away with it. I'm telling on you. You're really going to be sorry.

Me: I won't be sorry.

Izzy: Yes, you will. You'd better not call my mother a dumpster diver again.

Me: What do you want me to call her?

Izzy: Just call her my mother. She's my mother. And she has a name.

Me: (Laughing)

Izzy: Don't laugh at me.

At this point, Izzy stopped the role-play and asked me the following questions.

Izzy: Did the way I was handling it make you want to stop calling my mother and me dumpster divers?

Me: No. It made me want to do it even more.

Izzy: That's right. My anger made you want to continue and to escalate the insults. Did I make you respect me?

Me: No.

Izzy: Did I make you have more respect for my mother?

Me: No.

Izzy: In this game, who would you say was winning?

Me: I was.

Izzy: Were you having fun?

Me: Yes.

Izzy: That's right. You were even laughing by the end. Was I treating you like a friend or an enemy?

Me: An enemy.

Izzy: We are going to do it again, and this time I'm going to treat you like a friend. Insult my mother and me all you want. Go ahead.

Me: Your mother drives a garbage truck.

Izzy: Oh, you just found out?

Me: Yes.

Izzy: I thought everyone knew.

Me: She's just like you.

Izzy: Well, I'm too young to drive a garbage truck, but my mother does. How is my mother like me?

Me: Because you look like her.

Izzy: Thanks! My mother's beautiful.

Me: You always act like your mother, so you're a dumpster diver, just like your mother.

Izzy: My mother's wonderful. She works very hard in order to raise me.

Me: You're going to be a dumpster driver when you grow up, just like your mother.

Izzy: Actually, my mom is saving up money so I can go to medical school. She doesn't want me to drive a garbage truck when I grow up.

Me: Well, your mother isn't smart enough to do anything else.

Izzy: Some people think if you drive a garbage truck you have to be stupid. My mother does crossword puzzles in pen. And she actually gets paid a lot of money to take away your trash.

It became really hard for me to continue insulting Izzy. Then he asked the following questions:

Izzy: It looks like you've stopped putting me down. Are you having fun?

Me: No.

Izzy: Who's winning this time?

Me: You are.

Izzy: Do you respect me more this way?

Me: Yes.

Izzy: Can you respect my mother more?

Me: Yes.

Izzy: You see, you even respect my mother more this way even though I admit that she drives a garbage truck. I let you know how wonderful my mother is, and you start thinking, oh, maybe she isn't so bad after all.

Izzy then explained, "A kid in such a situation thinks their mother is being insulted because she drives a garbage truck. But the real reason is that the kid gets upset when her mother is insulted for driving a garbage truck. We all have things that can be made fun of. But it's our reaction that determines whether people will continue making fun of us.

"By the way, what I'm illustrating now is dealing with verbal attacks, but I also want to show how to deal with a physical attack. It doesn't happen so much with girls. Boys do a lot more hitting.

"Let's say you hit me. The natural thing for me to do is to hit you back, or to be afraid and run away.

"If I hit you back, you will probably hit me back even harder, and we may get into a big fight. If you're bigger and stronger than me, you may beat the crap out of me.

"On the other hand, if I'm afraid and run away, you automatically win. I give you power over me, and you will want to hit me every time you see me.

"So if you hit me, instead of hitting you back or running away, I will ask you, 'Are you mad at me?' I tell myself that if you hit me, you must have a very good reason. You must be mad at me. If you're not mad at me, you'll realize there's no good reason to hit me and you'll leave me alone.

"If you are mad at me, it means that you think I was mean to you in some way. Let's say that you and I are boys in high school and the reason you hit me was because you saw me talking to your girlfriend. It goes like this: Are you mad at me?"

Me: Yeah. You were talking to my girlfriend.

Izzy: Who's your girlfriend?

Me: You know.

Izzy: Sally? Sally's your girlfriend?

Me: Yeah.

Izzy: You're so lucky. She's so cute.

Me: Well, you're not supposed to think she's cute.

Izzy: Everybody thinks she's cute. She's like the cutest girl in the whole school. She's your girlfriend?

Me: Yes. So why were you talking to her?

Izzy: Because she's in my math class and we were talking about a test.

Me: I don't believe you.

Izzy: What do you think I was doing?

Me: I think you were hitting on her.

Izzy: Did it look like I was hitting on her?

Me: Yes.

Izzy: Okay, I'll try to be more careful. If she's yours, I'm not going to hit on her.

Me: Well, I'm going to hit you just in case. So you'll remember.

Izzy: Oh, don't worry. I'll remember. I'm not looking to mess with you. Anyway, do you think I'm going to take your girlfriend away from you?

Me: Yes.

Izzy: Look at you! You're an athlete and I'm a nerd. Do you think Sally's going to go for a guy like me?

Me: No.

Izzy: Of course not. Girls like that don't go for guys like me.

Me: Then why was she talking to you?

Izzy: Because, I'm a math whiz. We were talking about the test and I was going over the answers with her. She's not going to choose me over you. You have nothing to worry about.

Then Izzy explained, "You see, when I asked you 'Are you mad at me?' it changed the situation from a physical one to a verbal one. Instead of you continuing to hit me, we're now talking about it.

"I also want to explain about the word bully. People are most dangerous when they feel like they are victims. To me, you may seem like a bully because you are hitting me. But the real reason you are hitting me is because you felt victimized by me. You thought I was trying to take away your girlfriend, so of course you want to hit me. We call it bullying, but anyone who does something because they're angry is acting out the part of the victim. We only get angry with people when they do things against us. Anger is not bullying behavior, it's victim behavior. When you study psychotherapy, you learn that most people attack because they feel like victims. You may be angry because you feel you're not getting what you are entitled to. You may be angry because you're jealous that someone has more than you. Most people don't go around thinking, *I just love picking on people who are weaker than me. I can't wait to find someone weaker than me so I can hurt them.* Usually when we do something bad to somebody, it's because we feel victimized by them. So if someone is angry at us, we have to assume that they feel we've done something bad to them. So we should ask, 'Are you mad at me?'

And ask sincerely. You'll talk about it as friends and resolve the situation. But if you treat them like an enemy, then they'll act like an enemy and you won't resolve the situation."

I asked Izzy, "Would you have to go further and offer to help him with math as well?"

"Yes, I can offer to help if I want to. I'll treat him like a friend, and then rather than wanting to beat me up, he'll want to protect me.

"As I said before, the same people we call bullies are not only bullies. If we learn how to treat them like friends, they can become our buddies.

"Think about it. If I tell the teacher on you and you get sent to the principal's office, have I treated you like a friend?"

"No."

"That's right. And you're going to want to beat the crap out of me. If our parents are called in to the principal's office, your parents will be on your side and my parents will be on my side, so the principal has to play judge. A judge, at most, can only make one side happy. When a judge passes verdict in court, do you see both sides hugging the judge and thanking him for his/her wisdom? Both sides still hate each other. If the judge decided in my favor, I may love the judge, but now you hate the judge.

"If the principal took my side against you, you and your parents may now hate the school, too. Therefore, when the school gets in the middle of our problems, trying to help by judging who's right and who's wrong, it almost always makes the problem worse.

"That's why it's best for kids to be taught how to deal with their bullies on their own, without having to complain to the school authorities. Kids should go to the authorities for help either because it's an emergency situation, or because they want the authorities to teach them how to solve their problems with other kids on their own."

***

"Haters and bullies are always cowards, you know. They like to pick on little guys."

~Scylar Tyberius, *Sebastian the Great*

Vertically Challenged
by Walter G. Meyer

Walter G. Meyer is the author of Rounding Third and The Good from the Grief

***

Because my novel *Rounding Third* deals quite powerfully with teens being bullied until one of them can't take it anymore and attempts suicide, I have received numerous requests to comment on this timely topic. I have written about it for gay.com's *"Writes of Passage,"* the *Pittsburgh Post-Gazette, Rage Magazine,* and numerous other web sites. I have spoken about the crisis at Arizona State University, and the article about my talk was picked up by web sites all over the country. I have been a guest on radio and television shows to address the topic of bullying and suicide, including NPR in Pittsburgh, Channel 6 in San Diego, the Ask Dr. Annie Abrams radio show, and "The Week You Missed with Diane and Chris." In addition to speaking and writing about bullying, I also serve as an advisor on workplace bullying to Civility Partners, a consulting company. You can learn a great deal more about me, read many of my articles, find links to some of my appearances, and hear me reading from *Rounding Third* on my web site: http://waltergmeyer.com/bullying.html

Midway through elementary school, I seemed to fall behind my fellow students as they hit growth spurts and I failed to get mine. When the altar boys were lined up according to height for holy day processions at church, being the shortest, I always got to lead; even the boys who were several years behind me were taller than I was.

My lack of stature made me an easy target for the many bullies at that Catholic school. When George Bush's Secretary of Education, Rod Paige, suggested that the cure for school violence was posting the Ten Commandments in every classroom in America, I wrote him a letter pointing out that every classroom in my elementary school had them prominently displayed and that in no way discouraged the lunchtime beatings I got. My mother calling the school to complain only made things worse; I was berated by the nuns for telling on my fellow students. Clearly no help was coming from the administration. Often I would fake being sick to avoid going to school, and my parents had to bribe me to go. As I got picked on more and more, I became more fearful of making friends, which in turn made me an easier target and I fell behind socially as well as physically. The intimidation and harassment continued when I went to the public high school. Studies have shown that patterns established for the bully or target tend to follow them wherever they go for the rest of their lives.

Writing my novel *Rounding Third* was very cathartic; I cried writing parts of it and still cry when I re-read those parts. One of the elements I borrowed for the book from my own life was my fear that the nail that sticks up gets hammered down. I saw how the brainiacs who excelled academically got harassed for that. I knew I could do better in school, but, like the character in my book, chose not to get straight A's for fear of drawing more attention or harassment. I wonder how much better I could and would have done if I hadn't been afraid to excel.

I rarely made it through an entire day of classes in high school. I wouldn't skip class to smoke cigarettes or pot behind the school or in the cemetery across the street, as so many of my classmates did. I'd hide in a corner of the library or the office of the school newspaper. I was less likely to be attacked verbally or physically in my secret hideouts.

Luckily, I made one good friend in high school who convinced me that life could be very different when I went away to college, and it was. After a slow start my freshmen year, and fears I would fall back into the position of persecuted victim, I started writing for the school paper and soon gained the respect of many of the students and faculty.

But the scars lasted a long time. It took me years to want to assert myself.

The first really good friend I made after I moved to California committed suicide after we had been hanging out for quite a while. Years later, after I finally came out as a gay man by announcing it to the world in my annual holiday letter, among the recipients of that message was the mother of my late friend. She sent me her son's gold ring as a "coming out" gift, along with a note saying that her son was also gay and she wished he had been able to come to terms with who he was. It put a lot of things in perspective for me about our relationship. Sadly, he couldn't handle the societal pressure of hiding who he really was.

Rounding Third's main character, Rob, is an idealized version of me, the person I wish I had been in high school—if I'd found the courage to confront the bullies. I have since learned that often all it takes to stop a bully is to stand up to him. I don't mean in terms of challenging him to a fight. As small as I was, that was out of the question. Standing up in terms of asking why he felt the need to assault me. It has been shown that often just asking why is enough to stop the attack.

At an anti-bullying conference I attended, one of the speakers, Dr. Ron Holt, used a line I told him I was going to steal and use: "The bully will do what the crowd will tolerate." If the crowd eggs the bully on, things will escalate. If one person is willing to tell the bully to stop, and especially if more than one person says something, that is often enough to end the incident.

Many people who have read my book say it rings true for them and I respond, "That's because none of it's made up." It's a novel because the characters and the town are fiction, but everything that happens to them is true. It either happened to me or someone I know. I put together a mosaic of several people's lives to create these characters. A lot of people have told me that they experienced the same things that the boys in the book went through. Some have emailed to ask if I followed them around in high school because my recital of their teenage life was so accurate. It was a sort of validation to have struck a chord, but also rather sad that such tragic events are so common. And somehow it made me feel, retroactively, not so alone for having gone through what I did. I had felt, as so many others have told me they did, that they feared they had done something to deserve the ill treatment they got.

When I travel around the country speaking about my book and bullying, my talks can help serve as a mini-support group and make people aware of what can—and is—being done. There are so many more resources now, including web sites for groups like GLSEN and the Trevor Project, that, although students may still be harassed, at least they might not feel so alone. The ACLU, the Southern Poverty Law Center, and other groups are often willing to take legal action when school officials aren't doing their jobs and the parents are afraid or can't afford to sue.

When I speak, I carry with me the policies of the San Diego School District. I coordinated an anti-bullying event in San Diego with members of the school board and city council and was able to learn more about their policy. One key element is that it calls for counseling for both the bully and the victim. Often when they talk to the bully, they find his or her story as tragic as that of the victim: he is being beaten at home or she has a parent who drinks or does drugs, and the pent up aggression comes out at school. The policy calls for notification of the bully's parents. It calls for follow up with the victim and the bully. Too often, bullying is seen as a one-time event; if there is no tracking, the bully will step up the threats and punish the victim for getting them in trouble. It calls for mandatory reporting. Everyone—students, faculty, and staff—are required to report an incident. There is no such thing as a bystander. And each school has a designated person to whom all incidents are reported and who is responsible for follow up. Usually this is the principal, but, if not, another administrator is the go-to person. No longer is "I didn't know" an acceptable excuse. It is that person's job to know.

There is no one bully, or even a few, who stand out when I look back at high school. Just a nameless fog of a mob, many whose names I didn't even know at the time. In grade school, there were a few I knew well since the classes were so small. Although they caused me a lot of pain, stunted my emotional growth, and for a long time left me with a fear of trying new things and expanding my horizons, I don't harbor resentment. It serves no purpose. I can't go back and change what happened or how I reacted to it at the time.

With the reflection of years, I can look back and see that, on some level, their lives must have been more unhappy than mine, that they felt the need to bolster their weak egos by attacking me. I saw one of those bullies after I had finished college. He had dropped out and was still working the sort of job most of us gave up after high school. I didn't say anything. I have heard from many people who read my book that when they've encountered their persecutor(s) at reunions or elsewhere, the bully apologized and/or was stuck in a dead-end rut, unhappy and alone while the kid they had picked on had grown into a successful adult.

I was asked to speak about bullying to my old high school. It felt good and more than a little ironic that the quiet dweeb who was afraid to say two words when he went there was now addressing all fifteen hundred students in the gym about bullying. It may have been the first time the word gay was said in a positive way in that school. During the Q and A after, a student asked if I thought much about the kids who tormented me. I said I never thought about them at all. What would be the point? I can't change the past and I have moved so far beyond that scared little kid that it doesn't matter.

Section Eight

Cyberbullying

"There are students who are bullying both verbally and physically, and then cyber-bullying is another way to extend that by twenty percent. There is no respite now for kids. They don't have any way to get away from it. Students see their phones and the Internet as such an integral part of their lives and it's not something they can separate from or get away from. Students hide what's happening to them because they don't want their parents to cut them off from their social networking."
~Frank DiLallo, Author of *Peace 2 U*

***

"Tell your secrets to your journal. It won't betray you like a good friend turned bad."

~ Jill Ammon Vanderwood

Ask the Judge
by Tom Jacobs

I am a retired juvenile judge and the creator/moderator of AsktheJudge.info (http://www.askthejudge.info). AsktheJudge is a youth justice website answering teens' and parents' questions about the laws affecting minors. It is the only site of its kind answering hundreds of questions every month concerning laws and consequences for problems such as cyberbullying, sexting, smoking incense, and LGBT youth rights at school.

I'm also the author of the recently published book *Teen Cyberbullying Investigated: Where Do Your Rights End and Consequences Begin.*

Cyberbullying is a global epidemic because kids do it privately and they get away with it. This form of bullying is not like traditional bullying where people witness name calling or fighting. Kids who bully traditionally aren't as likely to get away with it. Cyberbullying includes cell phones and all the social networking sites. It's not just taking place when school is in session; it's 24/7. We have kids who write us every day because the issue of cyber speech is global. We just tell them, basically, think before you hit send. Think before you post or before you send that text message or before you sext a photo of yourself because states are cracking down on that sort of thing. Some of these actions have unfortunate consequences. There are adults who know exactly what they are doing in trying to entice a teen into a conversation online. One thing leads to another, and there have been tragedies that have come out of such contacts.

Parents need to be vigilant in monitoring their kids if their kids have an account on Facebook, Twitter, or any of the other sites. It's hard now because kids are so married to their phones. I know a lot of them who sleep with their cell phones. They don't want to miss that three a.m. text. According to the Cyberbullying Research Center, approximately twenty-seven percent of kids have been cyberbullied recently. They report that about seventeen percent say that they have been bullied and that they have also bullied people online. That's a huge percentage. It's too many to look the other way and ignore.

It's much harder to identify who's involved in this kind of bullying, and that's why there has been an increase in the number of so-called bullycides over the past few years. When a teen commits suicide, there's no way to know what was in his or her head at the last moment, but there's often evidence that the person was bullied, either online or over the phone. The ripple effect is enormous. It affects family, community, and friends. With media attention, these suicides are devastating even more people. Because the victim of the bullying chose that way out, because their pain caused them to take that final act, their torment has ended. But the suffering their suicide has caused their family and friends can go on for years.

The Trevor Project is the leading national organization providing crisis intervention and suicide prevention services to lesbian, gay, bisexual, transgender, and questioning youth. Jamey Rodemeyer was a fourteen-year-old bisexual who was bullied for a couple of years in middle school. His parents were aware of the bullying but thought it would get better when he began high school. Jamey decided to go public with being bisexual by posting a YouTube video to the It Gets Better Channel and posted comments on the Trevor Project site. The irony was that, after he came out, the bullying only got worse. His parents monitored him on Facebook and asked him how things were going; he said things were better, so they didn't really think there was a problem. On September 18th, he committed suicide. After he passed, his parents came to discover that he had other accounts on Formspring and Twitter. When they got into those accounts, they saw that he was being bullied online, and apparently that was what drove him to take his life. The fourteen-year-old from New York was buried in a Lady GaGa T-shirt. Lady GaGa has a song called *Born This Way*, and that was Jamey's motto. He would tell anybody, "Yeah, I was born this way. You have to accept me this way." When Lady GaGa heard that one of her biggest fans had committed suicide, she decided to channel her anger and pain into something useful. The Friday following his death, she dedicated one of her concerts to Jamey, and the following Sunday she met with President Obama and some of the cabinet members to talk about putting programs into public education to fight against all types of bullying. Lady Gaga and her mother, Cynthia Germanotta, have started the Born This Way Foundation, and quite a few high-profile celebrities have jumped on board in an effort to stop bullying.

Young people are killing themselves because of the intensity of the bullying they're experiencing. People may say, "This doesn't happen in our town," or "This doesn't happen in our schools," but they're just kidding themselves. It happens everywhere.

Imagine the pain of the person/people who caused the suicide.

Right. Exactly. You know, there's so much to it. We know these suicides are the in and that prompts legislators to take immediate steps and actions. Right now, out of the fifty states—fifty-one jurisdictions with the District of Columbia—there are only roughly ten states that have passed laws that actually use the word cyberbullying in the statute. Only ten, so far.

As a juvenile court judge, I observed the trends over the past fifteen years. As early as 1998 kids were starting to get into trouble for cyberbullying at school, and it was serious enough that some of them were disciplined by their schools and some were charged with crimes. The cases I saw in court involved the kids who were disciplined by the school and the parents disagreed with it. They would take legal action, and sometimes sue the school. Some won. It just depended on the facts in the case. That's the problem in this whole area of cyber speech, especially regarding students.

***

Here is a brief summary of how we get to where we are today. In the late 1960s, the Supreme Court looked at a few cases and, for the first time, they looked at teenagers and children as individuals. For the first time, they said, "Teenagers and children under the age of eighteen have legal rights; they are protected under the U.S. Constitution." The First Amendment includes a number of rights, and one of those is freedom of speech. There's a quote from a now-famous case: "Constitutional rights don't end at the schoolhouse gates," meaning that once the student steps onto school property and stays there for eight hours, they are protected both on and off campus.

The Supreme Court has addressed and ruled on dozens and dozens of cases about how far a student can go in trying to express himself, and how far the school can go with the discipline of a student. Both students and schools are always pushing the boundaries. Bringing the topic of freedom of expression up to today, the expression of free speech on the Internet is new to all the courts in the country. In my book *Cyberbullying Investigated*, I have laid out the shift change for the last ten years. I address how kids have gotten in trouble at home, at school, at work, and with the law over things they do online or with their cell phones.

I'll give you one case that took place a few years ago when MySpace was popular. A high school girl from Pennsylvania named Jill didn't like her principal, and she went on MySpace and made an account and a fake profile in his name. She went onto the school's website and got information, including his phone number, email address, and even got his picture from an area on the website where they had faculty staff photos. She added all this to his fake profile page. The comments she added to the page were sexual in nature, saying that he liked to do lewd things with teachers and parents. The school found out about the page and traced it back to her. Jill was suspended for ten days and the suspension showed up on her permanent school record.

It's a coincidence that in another case, which also occurred in the state of Pennsylvania, a boy who was a high school senior did the same thing. He didn't like his principal, so he took a picture from the yearbook and posted lewd comments on the school's website. The school didn't like it, and they suspended him for ten days as well. That went onto his school record and would affect him when he applied for colleges, scholarships, jobs, et cetera.

Both students fought the decisions and tried to get them overturned, and in the young man's case, the court determined that what he did constituted free speech. He did not do anything that was obscene or lewd, and the school should not have the right to discipline him. That cleared his record. The school disagreed and took it all the way to the federal court, but the school kept losing.

Jill and her parents challenged the school's action and, after years of litigation, succeeded. The federal court held that her posts, although inappropriate, failed to cause any disruption at school.

The two cases I just told you about are very similar, but they went to two different courts in the same state. There was a panel of judges who looked at the almost identical facts, and one court decided in favor of the school and the other one decided for the student. This happened because the courts have no guidance set by the highest court in the land, the Supreme Court, to define the limits of free speech for students. It's not absolute. None of us enjoy absolute freedom of speech under the First Amendment. There are limits. Hate speech, for example, or threats to do somebody harm are not free speech. You can be charged with a crime for certain kinds of speech. This applies to minors or students as well. That's kind of where we're at in terms of the law, and what's going on in this country.

Both of these cases were filed together before the Supreme Court because they came out of the same lower federal court, just below the Supreme Court. But in January, 2012 the Supreme Court decided not to rule on off campus free speech cases to address student's rights online. So at this point, these cases are still being decided by schools and federal courts.

The real question is can a school discipline a student who does something off campus? In most cyberbullying cases, they did these things at home, or in the young man's case, on his grandmother's computer at her home. They have done things away from school. If the school finds out about it, they discipline the student. So the question is how far can the school's authority reach beyond the campus? Can they reach a student's bedroom? And can the school reprimand them for what they do online and on their cell phones?

Take Action

I tell parents the etiquette lessons have to start at preschool age. Young children can begin to build trust with their parents or grandparents to report any online or text messages that don't make them feel good. Let them know that they should tell you. There are too many victims of cyberbullying who attempt suicide and survive—or don't survive— all because they didn't tell their parents. "No, I didn't tell my parents because I knew what they were going to do." Of course, parents love their children and want to protect them, so the first reaction is to turn off the computer or forbid access to the Facebook account. That's why kids don't tell their parents, and sometimes even siblings, because they don't want to lose their internet social connection.

I suggest that parents enter into a contract with their children regarding Facebook and other social networks and include in it: "If you are having trouble online, we need to talk about it. I will not take you off the computer and I will not take away your cell phone." This is a very responsible way for parents to act, even if it doesn't seem like it. It's a way in which teens will trust enough to tell.

In the case described earlier, the parents thought things were getting better because they were monitoring Facebook. But since their son had two other accounts that they *didn't* know about, there was really no way to protect him. They didn't know until they lost their son. His younger sister found him dead. Now his sister and parents talk to teens about cyberbullying.

What makes someone become a bully in the first place? If a child is raised in a home where they're exposed to a daily dose of domestic violence, they can bring it with them when they leave home and take it out on society. One percent of the teen population is involved in the juvenile court system. I spent twenty-three years in the juvenile and family courts, where I saw seventy-five families a week. Probably ninety percent of the kids I never saw again. Getting caught and having to come to court with a parent is usually enough to get most kids' attention. Only a small percent are repeat offenders, and those are the ones who make headlines. We don't hear about the ones who are out there doing good things because that's just boring. It's not our nature to seek a steady diet of positive news.

***

"When people hurt you over and over, think of them like sand paper. They may scratch and hurt you a bit, but in the end, you end up polished and they end up useless."

~Chris Colfer

Video Triggers a Hate Campaign
by Lauren Willey and Drew Garrett

Lauren Willey and Drew Garrett of San Luis Obispo, California, known as the Double Take Girls, wrote a song for their friends called Hot Problems. They were set up to film their short video through a friend. When the video went viral, they faced cyberbullying on an international level, but the biggest bully turned out to be the producer of the video and his father, who was a lawyer. The author interviewed the girls and Drew's mother, Annie, on a conference call.

***

Hot girls
We have problems, too
We're just like you except
We're hot (hot, hot, hot)
The world needs to
Open their eyes and
Realize we're not perfect
And sometimes we lie

Look at me
And tell me the truth
What do you do
When people don't know
What we go through

They see my blonde hair
Blue eyes and class
But they don't know
I have a really big heart

Don't get me wrong
I know that I'm hot
But textbook perfection
Really takes a lot

Where guys call my phone
And girls call me names

But Miley said
I can't be tamed

Hot girls
We have problems, too
We're just like you except
We're hot (hot, hot, hot)
The world needs to
Open their eyes and
Realize we're not perfect
And sometimes we lie

I got the look
I got the butt
But those things don't
Make me a sl--

Boys call me stuck-up
Girls say I'm conceited
On behalf of all hot girls
Those comments
Aren't needed

Just 'cause I'm pretty
I have to be dumb
I don't care about wits
I just wanna have fun

People start rumors and
Say things about me
Funny thing is that I didn't
Go to the party

Hot girls
We have problems, too
We're just like you except
We're hot (hot, hot, hot)
The world needs to
Open their eyes and
Realize we're not perfect
And sometimes we ...

Hot girls
We have problems, too
We're just like you except
We're hot (hot, hot, hot)
The world needs to
Open their eyes and
Realize we're not perfect
And sometimes we lie, ha!

Why, oh, why can't you see
You all are just like me
We make mistakes and get in trouble
Now you know our hot girls struggle

Hot girls
We have problems, too
We're just like you except
We're hot (hot, hot, hot)
The world needs to
Open their eyes and
Realize we're not perfect
And sometimes we

Hot girls
We have problems, too
We're just like you except
We're hot (hot, hot, hot)
The world needs to
Open their eyes and
Realize we're not perfect
And sometimes we lie.

Just kidding,
We're perfect

***

Lauren, how did you and Drew meet?
Drew and I met in middle school, but we didn't become close until
freshman year when we ran cross country together.

Who wrote the Hot Problems song?
We wrote the song together. It took about two hours.

What inspired you to write and perform the Hot Problems song?

Lauren: It was really just for fun and a joke. We just wanted to have a song to show our friends.

Drew: We wrote the song to begin with, and then a guy who went to our school was an aspiring film student, and decided he wanted to make a music video. We were like, "All right! Why not?"

Lauren: We just thought it would be funny, that's all.

Annie: Yeah, they had no idea they were going to become viral household names. That wasn't their intention at all.

Did you know you were going to put the video on YouTube?

Lauren: Not when we made it.

Drew: After the guy filmed it, he sent us a video link to YouTube. That was the first time we had seen the video. At that time, it was set on private so the only people who could see it were the people who had the link.

Lauren: After a few days, we all agreed that it could be public. We had no idea we should have signed an agreement so we would have a right to the video.

How long was it up before you realized that it was really popular?

Drew: The first day we put it out on YouTube, the Hot Problems video was super popular at school. Everybody started talking about it and posting it on Facebook and stuff. Then it went worldwide in a couple of days.

Annie: I'll give you the dates. Hot Problems went live on YouTube at 12:01 on Sunday, the 15th of April, and by Wednesday, April 18th, we were on a major FM radio station which goes to fifty-five radio stations in the U.S. and Canada. After that, the girls had appearances on CNN and MTV.

What was it like to go on national television?

Drew: Going on TV was a really good experience. By the time we were on national television, we had already done a few interviews by phone and on Skype, so we were a little more prepared. We were both pretty comfortable with the interviews and it was a lot of fun. We got to meet a lot of really cool people and the interviews led to other great opportunities.

It did happen really fast. How did you feel when people were saying that your song was the worst song ever?

Lauren: I thought it was awesome! If I actually thought we were good singers, I probably would have been crushed, but I just thought the amount of attention it was getting was super cool. I would rather it be the worst video than the second-worst video! The bottom line was to make people laugh, and we definitely did. To us, the video was a success.

Drew: I sort of agreed ... haha, to be honest, I knew it wasn't an amazing song. It was a joke, after all. If it made people laugh, I was happy with it. So when people said it was "the worst song ever," it didn't really bug me—at least they got some kind of enjoyment out of it. I mean, I'm honored people care enough about our song to talk about it!

Was most of the publicity positive or negative?

Lauren: Most of it was negative. In the beginning before anybody met us, it was extremely negative. And then when we started doing interviews and stuff, people figured out that we weren't actually being serious.

At first they thought that you were being really serious about it?

Lauren: Yeah, everybody took it super seriously in the beginning.

I could tell that it was supposed to be funny.

Drew: Yeah, we thought it would be obvious, too, but people didn't think it was so funny.

Annie: The only people who take it seriously are the people who don't have good self-esteem in the first place.

Did you start getting hate mail?

Drew: Yeah, we got death threats and stuff. Some of the death threats had to be turned over to the FBI.

Were the death threats coming through Facebook?

Annie: The threats were on the YouTube account. You hook up, or link, your YouTube account to your email account.

Lauren: We were bullied over Facebook, but not death threats.

Annie: When it got really crazy, they shut down their Facebook accounts for a while. They were getting friend requests and they didn't know who was who, so they stayed off Facebook for at least a week or two.

Drew: We have a lot of fans from other countries. Kids from Germany really, really like our video and they don't understand why Americans hate it. People in northern Europe really liked it as well. We have a lot of fans from Sweden, Norway, and England. I guess other countries have a different sense of humor, so that's probably why they like it more. Americans can be very judgmental.

But there were probably some people in the U.S. who liked it, weren't there?

Drew: Oh yeah, there definitely were, and when this was happening, Lauren and I were getting a lot of friend requests on Facebook. When we released the second video, we decided to accept all the friends so we could get the second video out there. So we added probably five hundred or more friends on Facebook. They would message us and say, "We love the video and we don't understand all the hate." Most of them were very cool about it. A lot were from other countries, but a lot were from America, too.

What kind of kids do you think would send death threats? Do you think they'd be the popular, hot kids, or do you think they'd be the kids who are threatened by hot kids?

Lauren: I think popular kids have self-esteem issues, too. Kids just get on their computers alone, so you never really know who it is. They are hiding behind the Internet.

Drew: Cyberbullying is almost worse than regular bullying, because everybody else can see the bullying on the Internet.

Yes, you could move to another state or another country and it would still be there.

Lauren: Yeah, and there are traces of it on there forever, too.

Did the FBI find anything?

Drew: We really don't know because we aren't in contact with the video producer, who made the report. We no longer work with them, so we don't get the death threats anymore from that video.

Lauren: I'm sure we still get them, but we aren't aware of them because they go to the YouTube account. The guy who set up the YouTube account won't talk to us.

Why won't he talk to you?

Drew: It's kind of a strange situation, I guess.

Annie: The producer became the biggest bully of them all.

Lauren: Yeah. It's a really big paradox. Personally, I wasn't affected by any of the cyberbullying because I couldn't care less about the names people call me. The worst person behind all of this has been the producer. He's trying to take everything from us and making it so the media can't get in touch with us. This guy wants to ruin our lives through this.

Wasn't he a friend in the first place?

Drew: I wouldn't consider him a friend. We went to high school with him. He was an acquaintance of ours. We knew him, but we wouldn't hang out with him on the weekends or anything.

Do you know why he's doing this?

Lauren: After the video got out, we were being playful and joking, but he seriously wanted to be discovered by the film industry. I think it hurt his ego because people weren't just criticizing Drew and me — there was negative criticism about the quality of the video as well. I think initially he was hurt by that. A week after the video went public, he said, "Lawyer up and don't contact me. I'm taking everything." The things people said about the video were nothing really, but if there was a reason why I wouldn't be sleeping at night, it would be because of him.

I hear that YouTube Videos that go viral can make a lot of money. If the producer is taking all of the money, do you plan to sue him?

Lauren: The producer's father is a lawyer, and I think they almost want us to sue because they know they have that advantage over us. Our parents are really against suing, plus it would cost money to sue them. I think he will probably get away with taking all the money. The rumor is that he's telling people it's forty grand, but we really don't know. It's hard to be the better person when you're being bullied on this level by someone else's parents, but our parents raised us to have good morals, so we try to keep it classy.

Are you working with another production company for your other videos?

Lauren: Yeah.

Annie: They are actually working with a production studio now. They are going into a recording studio tomorrow with a bigger, more well-known team, not just one college kid shooting the video. Tomorrow they start working on what hopefully will be a relationship for the next few songs.

You girls have the spotlight now, so you could accomplish a lot of things.

Drew: That's what we're trying to do. We want to use the opportunities that we have been receiving to not just benefit ourselves, but to help benefit others as well.

Lauren: Yes, we have a couple projects in the works and we are taking the positive out of this, too, and actually helping others.

Annie: The girls have a couple anti-bullying events with the YMCA along with the production company they are working with. It's funny, because we had no idea their new producer was already involved with an anti-bullying campaign. It was a fluke. He set the girls up to tell their story about bullying at his events in L.A. and Orange County. They will also start working with the Boys and Girls Clubs.

Drew: We talked with a family friend from Ohio. Their thirteen-year-old son committed suicide because he was bullied at school. The death just happened so the family isn't ready to do anything yet, but they know that we are trying to help them.

Annie: This is part of our mission statement against bullying. When a kid is only thirteen and the bullying is so terrible, they may think that suicide is the only way out. You don't have to commit suicide, because time will pass and it will get better. One of the messages that the girls want to get out there is that you don't have to take it personally. Mean things that are said about the girls are more of a reflection of the person who's saying it than it is on Drew or Lauren.

Have you ever been bullied in school? Were you popular in school?

Drew: Everyone gets bullied. Until about freshman year, I had funny-looking eyebrows that curled up on the ends, and I was really self-conscious about those. I didn't ever *really* get bullied, but I knew people talked about my eyebrows. I get along with everyone. I chose to surround myself with people I liked, who were nice and enjoyable, so it didn't really matter what "group" they were in. If someone nice sat next to me in class, we were friends.

Lauren: I have always had good friends, but I have been bullied before. It's almost just part of high school. Most of the bullying was on the Internet, but I have been yelled at and stuff on numerous occasions. One time I almost got beat up in a fight circle. I have also gotten things thrown at me a few times. My favorite was when someone threw a lollipop at me and yelled a bad word.

What were your favorite subjects in high school, and what are your plans now that you've graduated?

Drew: I was lucky enough to go to a high school that offered animal science classes. I studied large animal, small animal, and pre-vet, and I *loved* those classes. I'm going to be attending Santa Monica College in the fall—it's a community college. I'm going to do my general ed there so that I can transfer and study something in the Animal Science field. I may be a behaviorist or something.

Lauren: In high school I liked Social Studies-type things like history and government. I also really like to study languages like Spanish.

I'm going to San Diego State University in the fall to study International Business with a focus in Spanish as my second language.

Would you like to share a message about bullying?
Lauren: It sounds so cliché, but I just say don't let it get to you. At first, it was kind of hurtful when kids at my school were calling us dumb and conceited, but once it got worldwide, Drew and I realized that people said those things because that's what everyone else was saying. We know who we are and our friends know us.

Drew: The bullying will pass, so just have fun. Kids need to understand that it's not their fault if they are being bullied.

***

"I like people who I can occasionally have really deep conversations with, but also can joke around at the same time."
~Mariana Miller

Digital Citizenship
by Matt Ivester

Matt is the author of lol...OMG! What Every Student Needs to Know About Online Reputation Management, Digital Citizenship and Cyberbullying, and founder of Juicy Campus.com.

***

I graduated from Duke University with a double major in Economics and Computer Science. I'm currently pursuing my MBA at Stanford University, where I also serve as the Student Body Director of Digital Citizenship. Prior to business school, I held a number of positions, but the most notable and most relevant is that I ran JuicyCampus.com, the largest college gossip website in the country.

I was part of the first class of graduating seniors from Duke University that had access to Facebook while still in school. Digital cameras were common at that point, but cameras in cell phones hadn't gotten really useful yet. YouTube had only launched three months before my graduation, and Twitter wouldn't be founded until nearly a year after. I am just barely on the cusp of the generation that has been affected by the boom in social media and digital technologies while still in college. But that also means that I am part of the first class of students experiencing the real-world ramifications of our digital decisions in school. Combine this with my JuicyCampus experience, and I realized that I am uniquely positioned to write a book like mine.

Advice for Cyberbullies

It's easy to fall into behaviors online that, when you take a moment to step back and reflect on them, you realize don't portray the type of person that you want to be. If you've realized that you have been a part of cyberbullying, whether inadvertently or not, this is a good time to look at those behaviors and consider ending them. Your actions may have a serious and lasting impact on you and others.

The term anonymous is commonly misunderstood as meaning untraceable. All it really means is that your actions/comments/postings are unattributed; you don't have to sign your name next to them. A student at Loyola Marymount University found this out the hard way when he posted an anonymous shooting threat to JuicyCampus. Within hours, the police department had called me with a warrant that demanded the IP address, that unique number associated with every Internet-connected device, of the computer that made the post. A few hours after that, the student was arrested and charged with a felony.

JuicyCampus was not unique in keeping a record of IP addresses. All websites must capture your IP address in order to make their sites available to you, and almost all of them maintain a record of those addresses. Just because you say or do something anonymously online does not mean that no one will ever know that you did it.

All states have laws against harassment, and those laws can be, and have been, used to prosecute or punish people who use the Internet as a medium for harassment. In addition, states are increasingly amending their laws to explicitly address threatening, harassing, or bullying conduct online. These laws may impose criminal as well as civil liability. In California, for example, threatening to harm someone over the Internet can result in up to a year in prison. In Arizona, it is illegal, even for another minor, to send or possess an electronic message that includes sexually explicit images of a minor. And in Utah, it is a crime to make an electronic communication with the intent to "annoy, alarm, intimidate, offend, abuse, threaten, harass, frighten, or disrupt ...."

Advice for Victims

It's hard to know what to do when you feel like you are being cyberbullied. The first and most important thing to know, though, is that it is never really as bad as it seems at the time. It may seem as though no one understands, no one can help, and it's going to continue forever. But people do understand, can help, and it won't last forever, so, first, just take a breath and know that things will get better. Each situation is different and requires a unique approach, but the following basic guidelines should apply to most situations:

Consider the intent. If the person harassing you is your friend, or is a friend of a friend, or if you think there is any reason that the person may not be intentionally trying to cause you harm, there may be an alternate explanation for his or her behavior. Is it possible that you've misinterpreted what he or she has said or done? If not, is it possible that he or she may not realize the negative effect that his or her actions are having on you? Does the person consider this teasing all in good fun, without realizing that you don't? If so, you may be able to have a constructive conversation. You should consider contacting the person directly, and then calmly, non-accusatorily, explaining that what they are doing is hurting you. You don't have to explain why. Kindly, but directly, ask them to stop. If they decline, don't get into an argument with them. Just end the conversation.

Don't engage. If it is clear that the person cyberbullying you is doing so intentionally, it is best not to respond at all, even though it may sometimes be very tempting. Typically, responding only makes things worse. That's what the cyberbullies want. They want to upset you, to get a reaction. By ignoring them, you deny them that satisfaction, and, often, they will get bored and go away.

Keep a record. You may be embarrassed by the content that the bully is creating, whether it is in the form of messages, pictures, or videos. Or you may find them so upsetting that you simply don't want them on your computer or cell phone. Avoid the temptation to hit delete. You may need to use those messages, pictures, or videos as evidence. If you don't already have them on your computer, if they were posted online, or sent to your phone, take a screenshot or picture of it; just be sure to capture the message somehow.

Report it. You aren't an expert in how to deal with this stuff, and you shouldn't have to be. Report the offensive content to the website where it is occurring. Remember, all Facebook reports are anonymous. Then also report it to a trusted family member, administrator, or other authority figure. You don't have to deal with this alone.

Know the law. Specific laws vary from state to state, but if you are being threatened or harassed, that's illegal. If you aren't sure whether your situation qualifies, just ask. Local authorities, for example, campus police, are there to help. Together, you may decide that pursuing criminal charges makes sense.

Advice for Bystanders

Most students are neither victims nor bullies; however, with newsfeeds, commenting sections, and public tweets, many students do witness some degree of cyberbullying taking place during their school careers. Some may tell themselves that it is not their problem, while others may feel powerless to do anything. It is easy to come up with a reason not to get involved, but often, standing up and speaking out can have a really strong, positive impact.

Engaging the cyberbully online is not usually productive, and doing so may even result in you becoming their next target. But there are other ways that you may productively step in and help out. It doesn't have to be a big confrontation. If you notice that one of your friends is doing something that looks like cyberbullying, maybe you just casually mention, in person, that he or she should stop. Or if you see something online that you recognize as cyberbullying, you can be the one to report it to the site. And if you see something that's really serious, be the one to point it out to an authority figure. If your anonymity is a concern, go to someone you trust and ask him or her to keep your report confidential. Also, reaching out to the victim of the cyberbullying, offering your friendship and support, can mean a lot to that person and make a bad situation much more bearable. Little steps such as these can make a big difference.

How permanent is our digital footprint?

Digital content can last forever. Digital storage is now so cheap that it's practically free, which means there is no need to delete content. The comments you post online, the pictures you share on your blog, and the tweets you send out to the world may not always be at the top of your search results, but they will be out there somewhere for someone to find.

What can a person do to fix their reputation?

The most important thing when it comes to online reputation management is to own the results that show up on the first page when someone searches Google for your name. Ideally, all of the results would be about you, and they would be positive, showcasing the best aspects of your personality, interests, and abilities.

That's not always easy, though. It can take time and requires active management of your online presence. There are entire books dedicated to how to do this, but the two most basic steps are to create positive and neutral content about yourself—profiles on social media sites, blog posts, YouTube videos, et cetera—and then to crosslink that content— put a link to each of the other pieces of content on each page you create.

Why is it so important to protect our online reputation? We're only talking to our friends, after all.

A lot of students think that the content that they post online is only going to be seen by their friends. And for some people, that may be true 99.9 percent of the time. But it's that 0.1 percent that can really hurt you if you aren't careful. Like when you are applying to college and the admissions officer reads a joke out of context and thinks it's more offensive than funny, or when you are applying for a job and your boss decides that he or she doesn't want to hire someone who would go on an angry rant, cursing out people online.

***

"Someone who hates you normally hates you for one of three reasons: they either see you as a threat, they hate themselves, or they want to be you".

~Author Unknown

The Wrong Crowd
by Savanna Peterson

Savanna Peterson was cyberbullied when she was seventeen. She is the co-author of Drugs Make You Un-Smarter, along with her grandmother, Jill Ammon Vanderwood. She grew up in a family where she was exposed to drugs at an early age both by her father, who spent most of her young life in prison for drug-related crimes, and her older brother, who had parties with drugs and alcohol while her mother was at work. Savanna got involved with a crew of drug-free kids at age fourteen. She hung out with friends who shared her values of remaining drug free. What she didn't realize at first was that many of them were very angry and could be violent. After witnessing them beating younger kids just to steel their bikes, Savanna decided to leave the group, or unclaim. After she made that choice, the kids who had been her friends for the past three years turned on her and spread rumors on the Internet that she did drugs, among other things. Her mother's reaction was to take away Savanna's phone and keep her off the computer— not an unusual reaction from parents who want to protect their kids. But, remember, it is also a kid's reaction to keep such hurtful things as cyberbullying away from their parents because they fear their parents will disconnect them from their networks and what they see as their lifeline.

***

You were cyberbullied. Can you tell me how that started and why?
I was cyberbullied because I unclaimed from a crew of drug-free kids and I wrote a status on Facebook saying I'm not claiming this group anymore. A lot of people threatened me and made up rumors about me after that.

Why did you unclaim this group?
Because I realized that I was hanging out with the wrong crowd, and you don't have to label yourself to know that you can be drug free on your own.

Why would it bother anyone else if you made a decision for yourself?
It may be because later on they're going to decide the same thing. And people don't like it when people decide not to be something that they once were. I have talked to other kids who left this drug-free group and they say they are a lot happier and no one said or did anything to

them when they left. They usually stay friends with the same kids.

What kind of comments were you getting on Facebook?
They said things like "Kill yourself" and "You're a stupid slut," "I always knew you were going to sell out," and "You're going to turn out like your mother," et cetera.

What happened to you on Twitter?
They didn't think I was on Twitter, so they used my name, Savanna Peterson, as a hashtag and there were about six hundred tweets about me when I got into my Twitter account. Some people said they had nudes of me, some said they smoked crack with me. Quite a few people said, "Who is this girl, Savanna? I don't know her, but she's a loser." Some girls said, "It's a good thing Savanna doesn't have Twitter because she would have killed herself by now!"

What was going on that Sunday?
After I saw all the negative posts on Facebook, I was in a bad mood and I had been crying all day. My mom took away my phone and my iPad and told me to come out of my room and watch the Super Bowl with the family. We got into a huge fight, and my mom kicked me out of the house without any clothes or a phone. My grandma picked me up and we had to call the police to come and get my things. Mom wouldn't give me back my phone and told Grandma to keep me off the computer.

On Twitter, there were other things that happened that same day, and the trending topics were Number One: Savanna Peterson; Number Two: Josh Powell, who killed himself and his kids; and Number Three: The Super Bowl. I was talked about more than Josh Powell, which was kind of ridiculous because I didn't kill anybody. I just decided to go a separate way. I made a choice and other people didn't like it.

Did the bullying die down after that?
Not really. Some people will never give up on trying to make my life miserable. The only way I can avoid it is to just do my own thing and show them that they're not getting to me.

So what happened after you made your decision?
I kept changing my phone number, and somehow they kept getting it. I got late-night phone calls saying I was a sell-out and they were going to kill me. There was a broken window on my grandma's car, and I got jumped twice for my decision.

Tell me about being jumped. Where were you?

A guy I knew wouldn't stop sending hateful comments to me on Facebook. I deleted him, but he would write on someone else's status. He told this girl my age to beat me up if I went to a show. I wanted to go to the show anyway because my favorite band was playing. The guy who owns the business that puts on shows said I could go behind the counter and sell water so I would be protected. The whole time, only one person bought water from me. And I didn't even know that person.

I was with a girl I knew during the show and we went up to the front of the stage. Another girl just came up to my friend and hit her in the mouth while I moved out of the way, and I think it was me that was supposed to get hit.

So were you safe for the rest of the show?

After the show, I bought merchandise, and my guy friend told me to wait until everyone was gone before going outside. He was busy supervising and making sure things were packed up. When I went outside and looked around, everyone got quiet. I never made eye contact with the group of girls who were standing near the top of the steps, and they didn't look up when I walked by. I was just about to take my first step down the stairs when I got pushed from behind. My friend came out the door just after I was pushed and saw me fall, but he didn't see who pushed me. He said I flew, airborne, over twelve concrete steps. He ran down the steps and saw me lying on the ground, unconscious. He also saw a girl leaning over me, hitting and kicking me. I was unconscious, so there was no possible way I could fight back, or else I would have.

How did your friend get you out of there?

Everyone was just staring and laughing, and someone asked if I was dead. My friend had to push the girl off me, and he picked me up and put me in the car. Someone thought that he hit the girl who was leaning over me, and he said, "No, I had to get her off of Savanna."

Going in and out of consciousness, I sat in the car until my friend finished up and we could leave the show. I tried calling my grandma, but what I said didn't make much sense. Grandma talked to the guy I was with about taking me to the hospital and she met us there. I'm lucky for just having minor injuries as a result of this assault. I had a concussion, a black eye, and minor scrapes and bruises. She could have killed me! Some girl wrote on Facebook that I landed on her boyfriend's feet.

The police were called and they came to the hospital and asked me questions. They also questioned my friend. They took pictures and made a case, which was turned over to a detective. They found and questioned the girl, and she said I kept threatening to beat her up. She also said I was stomping on her feet with my high heels. She told the detective that she pushed me just to get me off her and didn't realize she was so close to the steps. All of that was a lie.

I started getting prank calls in the middle of the night from a blocked number. When I answered, someone would just yell "Sell-out!" One night I asked who it was, and she said her name. It was the girl who pushed me. I asked her why she lied to the police. She said, "Why do you think?" She said she was going to win because I don't have any friends and all of the witnesses are on her side.

Over the phone, I called her names, and she said she won. I said, "You pushed me from behind." She asked if I was going to Warp Tour. I said yes.

Around that time the window was broken on my grandma's car, showing that they knew where I live. The police said no other cars had windows broken on our street or any street around us.

What about your second attack?

I was at Warp Tour, and I brought my little sister because she'd never been to the concert before. At Warp Tour, there are bands from all over the country, playing from different stages all day long. I thought I was going to be okay because I had people who said they would protect me. Warp Tour is at the fairgrounds, so it's a large, open area. I got there and I tried to avoid crowds because most fights happen in crowded areas. I was standing on gravel listening to music and someone attacked me from behind, threw me to the ground, and started punching me in my face. I have no idea who pulled her off me, but she ran into the crowd. I didn't know who attacked me until the next day. This time I had my little sister as a witness.

The same guy who kept telling the other girl to fight me was standing nearby, clapping and cheering for the girl who attacked me. When we got home, my sister looked him up on Facebook, and then looked at his "friend" pictures until she found the picture of my attacker.

On Facebook, people I didn't even know were telling her how cool it was when she beat me up at Warp Tour. She didn't say one word to me when she attacked me. I knew this girl and the last time I talked to her, we were friends. I sold out, and she beat me up because I sold out. There's no explanation for what she did.

Did you make a police report about the second attack?

Yes, I reported the attack to the same detective who was handling my first case. I had two court cases and nothing was happening. I'm sure both of the girls were lying to the detective in each case. I had one witness for the second attack, which was my sister, but for the first one, everyone there hated me. The guy who took me into his car also turned against me. He said I had a bad attitude and he didn't want to help me.

I filled out a paper telling the detective the story about the attack. I was also asked what kind of restitution I wanted. I said I wanted them to pay for damages and pain and suffering. I was also asked if I wanted to know when the cases were settled and I said yes. I never heard anything more about the cases, but I'm sure they were settled.

What did you say to the first witness?
I just said, "Are you going to help me?" He said, "No, I'm scared. The last time I was a witness, I went to jail."

So he wouldn't tell them that the girl was hitting and kicking you after she pushed you down the steps?
No.

The last time somebody called you in the middle of the night, what did they say?
They said, "I'm going to kill you, your grandma, your little sister, and your stupid mom."
I said, "Okay, if you know my address, then come to my front door right now, and if you're not going to kill me, then that shows you're a coward." I also said, "If you don't do what you say you're going to do, then I'm not afraid of you, especially because of something that I decided to do with my life. And selling out was the best decision that I ever made. I'm happier and I don't have a label over me and I don't have to impress people by being aggressive and ignorant."

Do you think that the drug free people were too aggressive?
Yeah, their drug is to make other people miserable. They intimidate people just so they can feel better about themselves.

Do you think they intimidated the one witness you had?
Probably.
Let me tell you how I felt. When someone overpowers you and makes you feel like they won, you just don't know what else to do. You have bad thoughts, like you want to hurt them really bad to the point where they can't move. Being bullied is the worst thing anyone can do to you. I think someone putting you down makes you think about it over and over in your head to where it hurts as much as having surgery

or being hurt in a car accident. It's been proven that emotional pain is as bad as physical pain.

Do you still have physical pain from the attacks?

I still have a bump on my head, and my jaw pops out of place from when I fell on the concrete. I'm lucky I'm alive.

People were saying, "My name's Savanna and I didn't want to fight them so I just let them win!" I was seventeen and only five feet tall, and around a hundred lbs. Was it fair for some stupid guy to send girls to attack me from behind? How was I supposed to have eyes in the back of my head and know that they were going to attack me?

Advice for Kids:

If you are being cyberbullied, you can delete your social networks until things die down. You can block people on Facebook and go on with the rest of your life like it never happened. Just forget it! Think about other things. Keep yourself occupied with hobbies, sports, dancing, or school. Show the bullies that they aren't getting to you. They bully so they can make themselves feel better. They will stop when they find out you've moved on.

Do you feel better about yourself now?

Well, I get depressed sometimes, but things have died down. People don't bother me as much. I'm starting to show them how they treated me, and some people have started to apologize. They know I'm right. I have a strong opinion. I will never hold my tongue for someone who offends me or tries to offend me. Like Bob Marley says, "You can't point a finger if your hands are dirty." You can't judge somebody when you have problems, too. No one's perfect. People think I don't have power, but I do. The thing that I tell myself every day is "You're not made of glass. They can't break you. And you have a voice, so speak up!"

Section Nine

Celebrities Share
Their Stories About
Being Bullied

Celebrities Who Were Bullied

Information from Listal.com List of Celebrities Who Were Bullied

Christina Aguilara, singer, was never able to relate to other kids because she always wanted to be a star and be in front of a camera. She began acting as a cast member on the *New Mickey Mouse Club*. Once she had her tires slashed by classmates in high school.

Clay Aiken, American Idol finalist, told Dr. Phil he was bullied because he was the only male in the school choir. He didn't sing for a long time because of the taunting.

Jessica Alba, actress, was bullied because she was shy and awkward. Her dad had to walk her to school for protection, and she ate her lunch in the nurse's office.

Christian Bale, actor, began acting at age 13. He was instantly hated at school. Kids kicked and punched him at school every day.

Tyra Banks, super model, told a *GQ* reporter she was picked on at school because she was tall and skinny and had a high forehead.

Pierce Brosnan, actor and former James Bond, was teased because he moved to London with an Irish accent. This made him stand out among his classmates. He tried very hard to pick up the English accent.

Sandra Bullock, actress, was bullied because of the way she dressed and she was teased about her German mother.

Bill Clinton was the forty-second president of the United States. He was teased and beaten up because he was overweight as a kid. He was known as the Fat Band Boy.

Chris Colfer, actor, told *Rolling Stone* that when he was called names at school, he called the kids "delinquent" or some other words they couldn't understand. He told *The View* that he was bullied because of his voice. Now that he's famous, the same kids try to tell him they were his best friend in high school—but he has a good memory.

Tom Cruise, actor, was bullied for being small and not being able to read well because of dyslexia.

Miley Cyrus, actress and singer, became a star at a very young age and was bullied by the Anti-Miley Club at her school. Once she was locked in a bathroom during class by several girls larger than she was.

Jennifer Freeman, actress, was teased because she had a bad case of acne while growing up. Now she thinks the teasing made her a better person because she can understand what others are going through.

Lady Gaga, singer, was bullied in school because she stood out and she was different. On a recent episode of *Ellen*, she said that she wants her fans to know that it's okay to be different or feel like a freak. "Sometimes in life you don't always feel like a winner, but that doesn't mean you're not a winner."

Taylor Lautner, *Twilight* actor, told *Rolling Stone* that he was bullied in school because of his acting. He was determined to continue acting and tried not to let the comments get to him.

Demi Lavato, actress and singer, was targeted by mean girls in the seventh grade. The teasing became such a problem that she was home-schooled.

Kate Middleton, Duchess of Cambridge, was bullied in school. A group of girls stole her books. When she would sit down in the lunchroom, the others at the table would get up and choose another table, according to her former friend, Jessica Hay, in *Daily Mail*.

Robert Pattison, actor from *Twilight*, was beat up for behaving like an actor while he was in school.

Michael Phelps, world-champion Olympic swimmer, was teased for his long arms and legs, protruding ears, and a lisp. He also had ADHD, and a teacher said he wasn't gifted.

Daniel Radcliffe, actor from *Harry Potter*, told *The Mirror* that he was punched in the face by an older kid in school for defending another kid who was being bullied.

Jessica Simpson, singer, was a target for bullies because they didn't believe she had a record deal at age thirteen. Before the album came out, the record label went under. Some kids even threw toilet paper at her house and eggs at her door.

Brittany Snow, actress, was bullied daily and felt like an outcast in school. She was moved by the recent string of teen suicides to start the organization Love is Louder, along with the Jed Foundation and MTV. Love is Louder is a non-profit which is meant to bring awareness to bullying and depression.

Kristen Stewart, *Twilight* actress, was fine in school until, at age fourteen, some kids realized she was an actress. The bullying and name-calling got so bad that she continued her education through correspondence while focusing on her career.

Taylor Swift, singer/song writer, was bullied in junior high. She now realizes that the isolation and misery she endured because of bullying was the motivation for her to write songs.

Justin Timberlake, singer/actor, was bullied because he didn't play football. Taking classes in music and art made him stand out. Being different as a kid has helped him to be successful as a musician.

Michelle Trachtenberg, actress in *Harriet the Spy, Buffy the Vampire Slayer,* and *Gossip Girl*, was bullied in school. She was once thrown down a flight of stairs, fracturing her ribs and her nose. When she used the word bitch to describe the girl to the principal, she got detention, she told an interviewer for *Complex Magazine*.

Emma Watson, actress in the *Harry Potter* movies, dropped out of college for a while to avoid the bullying.

Kate Winslet, actress from *Titanic*, still gets bullied in Hollywood for gaining and losing weight. In school she was called chubby. People would say, "It's a shame she's chubby because she has such a pretty face."

Prince Harry Windsor was teased because of his red hair.

Tiger Woods, golf pro, was tied to a tree on his first day of kindergarten and taunted with racial slurs from older kids. He also suffered from a stutter, which he fought hard to overcome.

***

"When people see you're happy doing what you're doing, it sort of takes the power away from them to tease you about it."

~Wendy Mass, *Every Soul a Star*

Be the Best You Can Be
by James Donaldson

My name is James Donaldson, and I am a former NBA All-Star and recently published author of a book, *Standing Above the Crowd: Executing Your Game Plan to Be the Best You Can Be*. In my book, I write of the time when I was a teen and felt bullied and picked on, how it affected my self-esteem, and how I was able to deal with it and finally overcome it.

James, you say that you were bullied as a teen. Can you share the story here?

It's difficult being a young person or a teenager. Those of us who are past that period in our lives can appreciate all the things that young people and teenagers go through. Teasing, taunting, name-calling, being picked on, being made fun of, being excluded, and tremendous peer pressure are all part of the teenage experience.

I went through the very same things, compounded by the fact that I was self-conscious, insecure, and unsure of myself. I never felt a tremendous amount of peer pressure to do things that I knew weren't right, but that was mainly because I had very few friends and I knew better than to hang out with kids who would entice me to use drugs or join in gang activities. I guess that's the upside of being unpopular and not having a lot of friends.

I realize through reading about you that you were very tall for your age, overweight, and awkward. How tall were you as a teen? What was that like for you?

I came into this world at twenty-four inches and twelve pounds. I was six feet tall at twelve years of age and was wearing a size twelve shoe then, too. I was six-eight when I enrolled in high school, and was seven feet by the time I graduated, and then grew to seven-two by the time I graduated from Washington State University.

I was pretty self-conscious of my height by the time I got to high school. I just kept growing and growing, and feeling more and more embarrassed about it. I starting having to duck through doorways, squeeze into standard-sized school chairs and desks, and, plus, I couldn't wear the stylish fashions of the day. I never felt cool enough in high school to be one of the guys, so I slunk along the school hallways, hoping that no one would notice a seven-foot-tall classmate.

Do you know when the bullying started?

Yes, I realize when the bullying started, and, frankly, I was scared of these two guys in particular. It may have been an underlying reason why I didn't want to play basketball, even though my coaches and teachers encouraged me to do so. So, quite naturally, I just talked myself into thinking that I wasn't coordinated enough and I would never be good at it.

The bullying I experienced started when I was a sophomore/junior in high school.

Was it always the same kids who picked on you?

Yes, it was the same two or three guys on the basketball team. They were a year or two older than I was, and pretty accomplished basketball players, so they were sure of themselves, and at times pretty cocky. I got my first taste of being bullied as I was just beginning to express myself through sports. I was very late to the game of basketball—I didn't play my first organized game until I was a senior in high school—and that was mainly because of my lack of self-confidence and coordination.

I remember my basketball coach, Chuck Calhoun, as one of the very few people other than my parents who saw potential in me, especially in regards to basketball. As he gently encouraged me to pick up the game and start practicing during my junior year, I was met with a great amount of resistance and teasing in the locker room from some of the guys who were already on the team. A couple of the star players were threatened by the fact that I *did* have a great amount of potential, and feared I could possibly take away their opportunity to make a name for themselves.

These star players would pull a lot of pranks on me, and they weren't always reserved for the locker room. They would try to pull my pants down, or pull my shirt up, in the hallway in front of a lot of other students, threaten to spit on me, and pretend to snuff out their cigarette butts on my skin. Because I was shy and self-conscious of my overweight chubby body, I would do my best to keep myself wrapped in towels and do my undressing on the other side of the locker room so the guys wouldn't see me. I would even take a shower with my jock strap on. When the others saw me, they would poke and pinch me, many times painfully, when I was naked.

Now that I'm older, I realize there's a certain amount of hazing that goes on anytime you join a group or a team, be it athletic, a fraternity/sorority, the military, et cetera, and it's done in the spirit of initiating and welcoming you to the team. But, as we often see, it can go too far and get out of hand. These team initiations and hazing rituals can be very damaging to the self-esteem and confidence of the person who's under attack.

Did you have friends who would stand by you, even when others gave you a hard time?

Yes, the small handful of friends I did have were always my relief from the bullying that was going on. It was the basketball practices that I didn't look forward to.

Did you ever tell anyone that you were being bullied?

No, I never did tell anyone, and the bullying was one of the reasons why I almost talked myself out of a basketball career. I don't know if it would've helped or made things worse if I had told someone. It's not uncommon for people who are being bullied to start making excuses and rationalizations as to why they don't want to attempt or attend certain things. We'll find ways to cover up the fact that we're bullied by making excuses. "I don't feel like going to school because I'm sick." "I don't want to go to the high school dance because so-and-so isn't going to be there anyway." "I don't want to try out for the team because I'm afraid I might get hurt—or I'm not good enough." "I'm going to break up with my girlfriend before she finds out I'm useless." People who are bullied become experts at covering up the fact that they're being bullied.

It's a shameful, hidden secret that far too many young people carry with them, and it ultimately does nothing but negatively affect their self-esteem and their self-confidence.

How did you overcome your low self-esteem and realize you had potential as a basketball player?

I was very fortunate to have a wonderful mentor in Coach Chuck Calhoun. Even though he didn't know about the bullying that was going on behind his back, he took the time to make sure he helped me realize the potential that was buried deep within me. During my junior year, Coach Calhoun would cover up the windows in the high school gymnasium with newspaper and cardboard so the other kids couldn't peek in and scare me away. I was so uncomfortable with my abilities as a high school junior that my coach knew that, given the chance, I would've talked myself out of a basketball career. Remember, I was already making excuses—with the underlying reason being that I was being bullied—as to why I couldn't be a good basketball player in the first place.

Coach Calhoun was always making sure that my grades were up to par, and that I was going to be at basketball practice after school. He also suggested that I do extra running and weight lifting to start to build myself into the athlete that he knew I could become. If it wasn't for him taking the time to help me take the baby steps necessary in order for me to start working toward my goals and fulfilling my potential, who knows what would've happened to me.

How did you deal with the abuse?

The abuse and bullying that I experienced gradually started going away as I became a better basketball player. As I started having more to contribute to the team, I garnered more respect amongst the guys. Like I said, it's a painful initiation process that far too many young people have to go through, unfortunately, and unless they can figure out a way to deal with it in a positive manner, it can become very destructive. With my success in basketball, I gained more confidence, and I also started to become more popular in school.

You grew from an awkward kid to an NBA All-Star. What kind of dedication and leadership/coaching did it take for you to realize your full potential?

Coach Raveling at Washington State University knew that I was still pretty raw and green, but full of potential, and he took a chance on me by giving me an athletic scholarship to the university. Once I got there, he took a key to the weight room and the key to the basketball gymnasium off his key ring and told me, "Since I can't be with you twenty-four hours a day, seven days a week, these couple of keys are going to be a big part of the keys to your success in the future." He suggested that after my classes were finished, basketball practice was done, and I had myself a little bit of dinner, I should get back on campus and hit the weights and practice all the basketball drills he taught me during the day. I never forgot that advice. I kept those two keys with me and made my way back to campus every day. That was the beginning to my blossoming into a bona fide student athlete at Washington State University.

After graduation from Washington State University in 1979, the Seattle Supersonics drafted me into the NBA draft. I was being coached by Hall of Fame Player and Hall of Fame Coach Lenny Wilkens. Again, I felt like the baton was being handed off to another great mentor who really took the time to make sure that I was going to fulfill my potential. I don't think I could've broken in to the NBA with a better coach to prepare me for my long and prosperous career. Coach Wilkens treated all his players with respect, but also expected us to handle the responsibilities that we were given. I played my first three NBA years with the Seattle Supersonics, and I was very grateful to have Coach Wilkens as my coach and mentor.

When did you realize you had made it?

I don't know if I've ever realized that I've "made it," even after all these years. It reminds me of that old Satchel Page saying, "Don't look back ... because something's gaining on you."

I'm reminded of a very painful lesson I got at Washington State University. It was my senior year. I was one of the better players on the team—and we had a really good team. We went down to Los Angeles to play a weekend set of games against USC and UCLA. For one of the few times in Washington State's history, we were actually expected to win both games. I remember we got out there to play the first game, and we just got our butts handed to us—losing by about twenty-five points—and the player I was supposed to be guarding went off for a career night while I had one of the most horrible nights of my career. A couple of nights later, it was déjà vu. We lost again by about the same margin, and, again, the player I was supposed to be guarding went off for a career night, and, again, I had a horribly painful one. Assistant Coach Tom Pugliese came up to me after the games and point blank asked me, "James, do you realize what happened? Do you realize why you played such a horrible game?" And before I could even start to reel off my ready-made list of excuses—we all have them—he told me, "The players you were supposed to be guarding and the horrible games you played happened because *you became satisfied*." I never forgot that lesson, nor that embarrassment, and I have carried those three words with me—never be satisfied—everywhere I have gone and throughout everything I have done in my life.

So to answer your question, when did I feel like I had made it? I never feel like I have made it. I always feel like there's so much more to be done and there's a lot more that I could do to be better. That's not to say that I'm not happy or content with the list of accomplishments that I've been able to put together throughout my life, but I never want to be satisfied until that day comes when all is said and done and I can look back on my life and careers, and say, "Job well done! No regrets. Job well done."

For some people, living their dream and playing for the NBA would be enough. What drove you to run for mayor, go back to school and become a physical therapist, and open your own clinics?

Once I was able to come out of my shell and start to realize the vast pool of potential that I had inside of me, I actually started looking forward to pursuing interests that were, up until that time, only dreams, and, many times, things I would never have dreamed of doing, such as running for politics or becoming a businessperson.

So many young people have the potential to do and become just about anything they want to in this world. People need to listen to kids when they say they're being bullied so we don't risk them losing their self-esteem/confidence along the way.

Even though attempting some things in life or pursuing some dreams seem to be out of your reach, if you prepare yourself, study, and surround yourself with good mentors, you can accomplish every dream that you put out in front of you.

***

"Things will get easier, people's minds will change and you should be alive to see it."

~Ellen DeGeneres

Rise Above It
by Katherine Brooks

Katherine Brooks is a Hollywood director and producer.

***

I was bullied because I was gay in the small town of Covington, Louisiana. I ran away to L.A. when I was fifteen and lived in my car for six months.

I started having crushes on girls when I was very young, so I knew from an early age that something was different. I knew a lot of guys who were gay, but I didn't know of one lesbian. I didn't even have a role model who was lesbian.

When I was in high school, I fell in love with my best friend and decided to write her a letter about my feelings. I didn't really think it through. It was one of those moments where I felt like everything in my life had led up to that point. I just knew she needed to know my true feelings. My best friend showed the letter to some girls in our class, and, before the week was over, the entire school was aware of my feelings. I was treated horribly. There were obscenities written on the outside of my locker, people laughed at me, and my friends wouldn't talk to me anymore. It was devastating.

Dealing with My Feelings

I thought I was worthless. I almost believed everything that was said to me. I even believed that I was fat, even though I was an athlete. People don't realize how much their words can really hurt.

I literally grabbed the cash I had and stuffed a change of clothes in a small backpack. I didn't think about packing more clothes or food, and I didn't know exactly where I was going until I got into the right frame of mind. Then I just said "Screw it!" and drove to Hollywood. I had just enough money to get there.

I told my parents I was leaving, but they didn't think I really meant it until I called them collect from Los Angeles. My mom and dad were going through a divorce, so they were busy with their own drama. At the time, I didn't tell them the reason I ran away.

I'd started driving around my parents' property when I was only eight years old, so my parents got me a car when I was fourteen.

I lived in my car in the parking lot of a Hollywood motel. Nowhere is safe for a fifteen-year-old girl alone in a car. But a place like L.A. is really tough. I was afraid I would be raped, and it almost happened.

By the time I called my parents from Los Angeles, I was a good actress and lied to them about my situation so they wouldn't worry. No one turned me in for being a runaway because I looked much older than my age.

At first, I survived by asking for money from strangers. I also got enough money to get a YMCA membership, so I used the gym to shower and washed my clothes in the sink.

I lived out of my car for six months. I got my GED and worked odd jobs until I was able to find a job where I could use my training as an equestrian. My new home was in a Malibu stable, where I gave guided tours on horseback.

I waited a few years before I went home for the first time. It was strange to be back. My family and I are very close now. My family has always been supportive of my dreams, even if they didn't agree with how I went about achieving them.

Have you seen the people who treated you so badly in high school?

Yes, I have been back, and people are much different toward me now. I guess things have changed in the small town. They are kind to me. I think they are impressed with how my life turned out.

I have lived in Los Angeles for twenty years. Being in a bigger city has made my life much easier as a gay person. In L.A., it's not as taboo.

I now have a career as a film director and producer.

You said that you didn't finish high school. Can you tell about the career path you took and the hard work you went through to become a director and producer?

I always knew I wanted to make movies. Always. At some point, I wanted to be an actress. I started out being an extra for film and TV. It was not so bad, but you are treated like cattle. I quickly realized that I was more of a storyteller than an actress.

From there, I got a job as a camera assistant, and in the meantime was also shooting my own short films. I was able to get one of those films in the hands of my executive producer, and he gave me a shot directing *The Osbornes*.

You have come a long way since leaving home at age fifteen. How did you go from running away to being a movie producer?

It took a lot of hard work and determination and never taking no for an answer.

I believe we create our own reality and that we can do anything we put our minds to. I refused to let people tell me I wasn't good enough.

We want kids to know that they, too, can find their place in society, no matter what is thrown at them along the way. What advice would you give kids who are being bullied?
All of the amazing people in this world were bullied at some point. You have to know deep down that you are special and unique and have something to offer. You have to know that bullies are just cowards and have low self-worth. Rise above it and know that you are better than that.

***

"He who believes is strong; he who doubts is weak. Strong convictions precede great actions."

~Louisa May Alcott

Show Them You're
Strong and Healthy
by Heba Salama

Heba Salama, winner of The Biggest Loser, makes appearances at national conferences around the country, including the American Heart Association and Children's Center for the Physically Disabled, and appeared in The Biggest Loser Workout DVD. Here is her website http://www.edandheba.com/. Heba and her husband, Ed, entered The Biggest Loser as a couple.

At the beginning of the show, Heba was wearing a size 24 and she weighed two hundred and ninety-four pounds. At the end of the show, she was the Biggest Loser, losing one hundred and thirty-eight pounds. The couple lost a combined total of two hundred and seventy-five pounds.

***

Heba, congratulations on your and Ed's success on *The Biggest Loser*. I hear that you were bullied while you were in school. Do you know why?

I was most likely bullied for being heavier, taller, and louder than most people growing up.

Did you become louder for attention, or did you have great self-esteem?

I had great self-esteem, meaning that I was a happy person. I always made the jokes about myself first; I was always loud and loved attention—always!

Do you know when the bullying started?

I clearly recall the first time was in third grade. I got teased about my name *a lot*.

What is the origin of your name?

My father is Egyptian.

What kind of student were you?

I was an A and B student. I came from a family of academics, so it was important to make good grades.

Were you popular in school? Did you join clubs, sing in the choir, run for student body office, or try out for school plays?

I performed in school plays and chorus. I had lots of friends. I would say I was friends with the popular and athletic crowd, but wasn't the captain of the cheerleading team. I was a great friend to many people and was also the funny friend.

Were there kids who stood by you, even when others were cruel?

Yes, I always had friends, and I am friends with them still to this day. I am even good friends with a lot of the bullies.

How long did the bullying continue?

This continued into high school. I was always well-liked and had friends, but it was *easy* to single me out.

Were you always overweight? Was this an issue at home as well as at school?

I was always tall and overweight. My weight problem got worse when I went to college. My mother said more about it than my dad. He supported me at any size.

How did the bullying make you feel? And what did it do to your self-esteem?

I think I was always confident despite the hurdles. It hurt to be bullied, but it didn't break me down or shatter me. I liked a challenge, and often figured I could kill them with kindness, which I know is unusual.

How did you reconcile the differences with the bullies to become friends?

I received multiple apologies from different bullies. I hate even using that word now because I have a lot of respect for the fact that a good portion of the people who picked on me have stayed in my life, and are some of my greatest friends to this day. Sometimes the topic comes up even now. Although I wouldn't wish it on anyone, I think it made me the person I am today. It made me a fighter.

Can you tell about your success on The Biggest Loser and how this has changed your life and Ed's?

We feel more in control, not afraid of a challenge or anything in life. It instilled a new confidence, and gave us our freedom by not having to feel trapped by our weight. We have kept the weight off, and now I like to talk with kids about making healthy food choices, working out a few hours a day, and having a healthy balance to life. If we could stop any teenager from having to go through what we went through, it's worth it.

If a kid is being picked on because of their weight, how would you encourage them to keep going?

Just look toward the future. It gets better and you will be better for it. Take your anger out on a run, and show them you are strong and happy.

***

"Never be bullied into silence. Never allow yourself to be made a victim. Accept no one's definition of your life; define yourself."

~Robert Frost

They No Longer Have Power Over Me
by Daniel Joseph Baker

When Daniel Joseph Baker performed "Bad Romance" by Lady Gaga on the stage of America's Got Talent, the judges' comments included "He is this generation's Liberace." On national TV, he told about being bullied throughout his school years. He began performing in church and at school talent shows at age six. Bullying and changing schools several times left him with little or no confidence. In the few years leading up to his audition, Daniel would only perform in his own living room. Trying out for America's Got Talent on a whim brought Daniel Joseph Baker into the limelight, allowing him to see the true star that he always was. He was a semi-finalist in the one of the largest talent shows in the nation. After his last performance on AGT, he made the comment, "I feel the best I've ever felt in my life and I know there are only good things ahead for me."

***

Daniel, can you tell about being bullied?

Being bullied every single day from the second grade on was a terrible thing and shaped me for life. Each school year, the taunts, harassment, and insults became worse. And, honestly, since I became an adult, I now wonder what happened to those children that made them become bullies. What did their parents do wrong? I can now feel bad for those bullies.

Do you know when it started?

It started when I was around seven. At recess, the boys would tell me to go play with the girls since I acted so much like a girl anyway. They said that since I was a girl, I wasn't allowed to play with them.

Was it always the same kids who picked on you?

Yes, most of the bullies were repeat offenders, and the group just got bigger and bigger as I aged. I knew all my bullies by name during those years. Luckily, I no longer remember their names now, so they don't get to have that power anymore.

Did you ever tell anyone? Did that help or make things worse?

I told my friends and my parents. When I was younger, though, my friends were all bystanders and wouldn't stand up for me. I don't blame them now, but being a bystander is the worst thing you can be. Someone completely not involved has the power to go tell someone and empower the victim.

I also told my parents, who absolutely knew I was having a hard time. I am very grateful that they have always stood by me. They documented each time I came home saying I got bullied and they went to my school principals many times, trying to make sure it didn't happen again. However, the principals would suggest that I switch classes or just handle it with the bullies and not bring it to the next level. My parents did everything they knew how to make the bullying stop. But, ultimately, if the school administration won't work with parents, there comes a point when nothing else can be done. I feel that if the bullies were reprimanded, it would have sent a message that what they did was wrong.

Were you ever cyberbullied?

No, growing up I was never cyberbullied because social networking wasn't as big then. However, in my adult life I have been cyberbullied. People will say horrible things from behind a computer screen, all to make themselves feel better.

When you were young, did you ever try to share your talents?

My mom is a trained opera singer, and she really wanted to pass on her singing talents to one of her children. I was the chosen one, and I'm so glad!

Starting at the age of six, I was performing regularly at church events including baptisms, sacrament meetings, and talent shows.

What kind of problems has bullying caused in your life?

It wasn't until recently that I realized just how much who I am today has stemmed from being a victim of bullying. My biggest challenge was getting over the feeling of being worthless. Bullying striped me of all confidence and made me feel like I was the cause of my own bullying because I was such a freak. I no longer think I'm a freak, but I still work every day to get over feeling like I don't matter and that I don't belong.

Did you ever have the courage to stand up to the bullies?

I never had the courage to stand up to bullies while I was growing up. I always walked away, hoping they would stop if they didn't get a reaction out of me. I just wanted the bullying to end. I could pretend to ignore the taunts, but later I'd cry around my friends.

How did you get the courage to go on *America's Got Talent*?

Sadly, I didn't audition for *America's Got Talent* out of courage. I auditioned out of unhappiness about where my life was at that point. I was tired of shady friends. I was tired of studying political science in college. I was tired of not feeling fulfilled in life. I knew I was born to perform, but I had lost all my confidence. *America's Got Talent* was a last resort, and I auditioned on a whim. I knew I needed to break away from my unhappy life, and I was hoping the show would do that for me.

What difference has your experience on *America's Got Talent* made in your life?

Being a finalist absolutely changed my life. Before AGT, the only place I performed was in my living room. Now I perform all over the country and have loyal fans who love me. Before, I never had the confidence to refer to myself as a singer; I never thought I was good enough. Now, I love introducing myself as a singer. The list could go on and on, but basically everything I'm doing right now, I never thought I could or would be doing before AGT.

What are some of the things you are doing right now?

I have performed at a benefit for the L.A. Children's Hospital, an AIDs event in Knoxville, sang the National Anthem for the L.A. Clippers game, performed at schools around the country, private parties, and much more.

Daniel, you are a great example for kids who are being bullied.

I do take my responsibility as a role model very seriously. I want to be a voice to inspire kids and show them that there's light at the end of the tunnel and that I'm living proof of that. No matter how long your tunnel is, you will always end up seeing the light of day.

***

"The bullying was hideous and relentless, and we turned it round by making ourselves celebrities."

~Julian Clary

My Awakening
by John Wright

John Wright is an international model, movie producer, and actor.

***

I experienced bullying when I was young, as well as when I was a teenager. Even as an adult, I have occasionally experienced bullying in everyday life. It's a terrible thing. In 2002, I worked with the Canadian Government to help develop anti-bullying education in school systems.

A Sensitive Kid

I was a very sensitive kid, and would be sad if I saw someone being hurt. For example, I witnessed a kid making fun of an overweight kid, and it made me cry. I was quite tall for my age and this may have made me a target. Two kids picked me out to beat up every day on my way to school. It was awful for me, though at that age I didn't understand why at other times these same bullies would seem to be my friends. One of these kids, named Joe, was troubled. He was one of the first kids I heard listening to rap music with swearing—at age seven. Back then, that was crazy. I think he was just a bully to anyone who bothered him or disagreed with him.

I learned years later that Joe became the head of a nasty Persian gang and was murdered in a movie theater. The event was highly publicized.

Joe's death impacted me because I knew him, and although he bullied me on occasion, we were also somewhat friends during my early childhood. I now see where violence can take someone when it is with them from a young age.

Changes At Home

My mom was a single parent and I was her only child. When I was ten, she married my stepdad. Not only did I experience serious changes in my household, but this led to our moving when I was fourteen and again when I was fifteen. My two little brothers were born, and, with each birth, we needed a bigger house.

I had tons of friends before we moved; I was more the leader of the pack. I would come up with ideas and friends usually followed me. My big ideas included buying surplus Army gear and playing in the forest or riding our bikes from N. Van to Vancouver. But upon moving, that all changed. It became harder to make friends. I was now a teenager moving into a new school. I had never had to try to make friends before. Just when I started making friends at the new school, we moved again. I was lonely and that must have showed, so people would pick on me, saying things like, "Don't you have any friends? Haha!"

I was shy, kind, and a very easy target. I was also quite big, but I would not fight back, so beating me was easy and improved their standing with their friends, as they just beat a tall dude.

Trying to Fit In

Not having friends meant hanging around with misfits, and these were the kids who drank booze and did drugs. I would say in my case that bullying led me to drugs and alcohol. I learned to drown my social anxiety in alcohol and drugs from age fifteen to twenty-six.

In high school, when the bullying became worse, I stood up for myself. If someone started to bully me, I would hit them. Since I'm tall and quite strong, it was very effective. I would also stand up for other kids who got picked on. Basically, I was a threat to bullies because I fought back and took on the fight for the picked-on kids. When I played rugby, there was a kid who was very strong and big, and he always pushed me around. I couldn't stand up and fight back, because he was several years older, in grade twelve when I was in tenth, and he was enormous and very strong. He would shove me to the ground, or hit me. If I stood up to him, he would try to stomp on me with cleated shoes.

The Consequences of Bullying

During a tough phase of my life, feeling suicidal, I ran away from home. A girl invited me and a friend her home while her parents were out of town. There were only derelict kids in the house, and we were playing with her parents' shotguns. I remember my mental state and how I had been affected by the big bully from my high school. On a whim, I packed a loaded weapon in a duffle bag and went out with the intent of murdering him. I was out of my mind from drinking and drugs. He was nowhere to be found, thank God. But that's an example of the drastic levels bullying can drive someone to.

Ironically, I ran into him years later. He'd became a guitar tutor. We talked amiably, and he even offered me lessons. I had no more hatred toward him. It's amazing how people change.

Bringing Down Youth Crime Rates

A few years after high school, having a few minor run-ins with the law, I was sought out by a man named Ben King who worked with the

Canadian youth in our town. He had a government grant and wanted to hire "badass" youth and give them direction by getting them involved with the community. It was a small town, so everybody knew everybody. When the grant idea came up, my mom called King and asked if they'd interview me.

During the interview, there was the question of whether I was using drugs, which I would not admit. I did very well in the interview, since I had learned to stand up for myself. I'd become very confident, and that shone through. They loved me at the interview and hired me. The hired youth were paid a salary and asked to develop and implement programs aimed at helping kids with issues of bullying, employment, and other things. Because we were young and considered cool by the youth in the community, we were widely accepted and had a great impact. We were given access to resources such as the mayor's office, the police, fire department, and leisure service activity facilities. I ended up leading our group and setting up seminars for grades K through seven in school gymnasiums about many issues, including bullying. We succeeded at bringing down crime rates and bringing up community involvement.

On My Way to College

I had a serious drug and alcohol problem, but I was inspired to go to University by Ben King, who became a role model to me. He had his Bachelors from Simon Fraser University, so I went there as a psychology major. My goal was to help people. With the pressure of working two jobs, a full-time school schedule, plus studying and girlfriends, my drinking got heavier. Next I got into ecstasy and cocaine, and my problems got worse and worse. I was sought out and hired by the government of BC, Canada, and took the job full time. At that point, I couldn't manage life anymore—I was drinking every night, doing drugs every other night, and missing work while my grades at school were dropping. I ended up taking a semester off school and got in trouble for my drinking at work at the same time.

Then Something Strange Happened

All of a sudden, I was hit with the overwhelming feeling that I needed to do something big. I was sitting in my messy apartment, looking at the TV set, and I saw the world in a way I'd never seen it before. I realized that all the coffee shops that were becoming popular had something to do with the TV show *Friends*, and all the catch phrases of the day came from TV, too. Even the clothing and style trends came from the illusive Hollywood. My college major was psychology because I wanted to help people, but I knew I couldn't help people in the state I was in. I needed to get involved with television and film. TV is the most influential thing on the planet. After that, I went back to my job and quit immediately. They thought I was crazy.

A New Career Takes Off

I walked into a top talent agency without a resume. The receptionist laughed out loud at me and kept laughing. I didn't even have a headshot. The owner of the agency heard her and came out. She had me read some lines and signed me. The receptionist's jaw dropped.

The next thing I had to deal with was my stage fright. I couldn't even read out loud in high school—I would faint. So I took an acting class and I still fainted the first few times I had to do a monologue or a scene. I passed right out on the floor, but I didn't quit. After a few months of building trust with the class, I was able to perform and remain conscious.

This was my life turnaround. My government supervisor offered me my job back if I went to drug/alcohol treatment, at their expense. I said yes as a means of getting treatment—I would have *never* considered that I needed treatment before. So I cleaned up and booked my first audition in a feature film, booked some TV commercials, and wrote a script and shot a film. I shot my own feature film, on a whim, with no training at all and no budget. The film made it into the Cannes Film Festival. I was signed as a model at the same time and sent to Milan, Italy. I took a short break from my modeling job and drove down to Cannes for my film. I met Beyoncé, Minnie Driver, Karl Lagerfeld, Claudia Schiffer, Coolio, Brad Pitt, Angelina Jolie, and Leonardo DiCaprio.

***

"Be great in your life and become as bright as the stars in the sky. But be patient because every star will have its time to shine."
~Timothy Pina, *Bullying Ben*

Your Own Place in this World
by Kristen Dalton

Kristen Dalton is a model, actress, producer, artist, and comedian.

***

I began modeling when I was sixteen years old and later made the shift into acting and producing. However, my beginnings were anything but glamorous. "Gumby" was the name I had been given by most of the kids at my school. It was difficult for me to smile without exposing my gums, which would almost always conjure up "Gumby" from the mouths of my comrades. I eventually determined to erase smiling from my register of facial expressions. Kids would make it a goal to elicit a smile from me so they could then laugh, tease and call me Gumby.

Later on, following a surprising turn of events, I fell into the world of modeling. One of the first jobs I got when I went to Paris was for a toothpaste campaign. I had trained my upper lip not to move too far up when I smiled. I eventually graduated to commercials, shooting over two hundred, as well as a plethora of editorials, catalogs, and campaigns. It would seem like poetic justice had been served considering the nucleus of my success was rooted in my once ridiculed smile. This evolution gifted me a great deal of confidence and catharsis. It was healing.

In middle school, the bullying had evolved at the expense of my sensitivity. It was less than a challenge for my classmates to bring me to tears. To make my point, I will say that "effortless" would be the more appropriate adjective. This time around my nickname was "Cry baby." The favorite pastime of my classmates was to make me cry. I think that's kind of sad. Every day I would tell myself, "Today I'm not going to cry, no matter what. Nobody can make me cry." This daily mantra seemed to have very little success, because I would always cry. Working as an actress now, I'm required to cry on cue, so it worked out in the end, I guess.

In high school, there was one particularly motivated bully. She used her free time putting ads in the local Manhattan Beach *Beach Reporter*. The stories and claims that were made in regards to me were entirely false and in poor taste. One ad was a borderline threat in which she warned me to "Watch out!"

Yet again I was granted another taste of poetic justice further down the road. I ran a restaurant/club with a boyfriend at the time and one night she just so happened to waltz into my establishment. It was the type of place where there was always a line. You could register your car quicker at the DMV than you would be able to score a table at my restaurant. I figured I should let bygones be bygones. I went to the maître d', a dining-room attendant who is in charge of seating customers, and I said, "Why don't you go ahead and give her my table so she doesn't have to wait." I then walked up to her and said, "Hey, Paula, it's me, Kristen." She gave me a blank stare and I said "I knew you from high school, and I just wanted to—" I was going to say that I just wanted to give her my table because I had a table every night.

She said, "I don't go to high school anymore," then turned and walked away. So I went back to the maître d' and said, "I'm going to keep my table. Just let her keep her place in line."

I wanted to believe that when entering adulthood, people progressed and changed for the better. After that encounter, I knew there was no resolution with her.

I have had run-ins with several other bullies since my school years and I really didn't need to say anything because I felt like I was living a successful and happy life. There was one girl in particular that I encountered years after her bullying days. In this case I acknowledged her by saying hello. She had graduated to weighing a few hundred pounds and she began telling me of the various tragedies in her life along with the degree of misery with which she was shackled. I was cordial and kind to her. At that point, I felt she had suffered enough and that it wasn't necessary to confront her with the bullying from her past.

Did you have anybody who stood by you in school when you were being bullied so much?

I had different friends at different periods of time. My best friend from seventh grade turned on me the following year in eighth grade after becoming friends with the pseudo-popular group. I was quite upset about that. This seemed to be a recurring pattern whenever I made friends. The one truly loyal and authentic friend I had happened to be the only African-American boy at my school. He was my buddy. He even ended up being one of my bridesmaids at my wedding, despite his heterosexual orientation.

How did you get the confidence to be a model and an actress? After being bullied so much, it would be hard for you to even open up your mouth and smile.

True, and I was very, very shy. I would fall apart around kids my own age, but around adults, I was good.

I was pushed very hard by my parents to get good grades in school. My stepfather used to have me do big stock portfolios on the computer. Dinner would not be served at the table until I could recite my times tables forward and backward at rapid fire speeds. This of course put me at the top of my math class.

During the summer I started working. I started out cleaning tables for my mother's company, which catered company picnics. By the ages of twelve to thirteen, I knew the catering job better than everybody else. By the time I was fourteen, my mom had me supervising. And when I turned fifteen, I was driving and supervising up to fifteen people who worked under me. I think working was a major contribution in boosting my confidence.

When I was in fifth grade, I started working for my stepfather's company during the winter months, assembling computer memory boards and cables. I had to do thirty or sixty memory boards a week. One day I happened to discover that the illegal immigrants working for his company were getting thirty dollars for each memory board, while I was getting a measly six dollars. Nonetheless, I was still making good money for my age.

How did you "fall" into a modeling career?

While working for my stepfather, a guy I knew asked to take pictures of me. I just assumed he was crazy. He had ambitions to become a photographer for the Elite Model Management Agency. My girlfriend helped with my makeup and he took my picture for his portfolio. When an agent saw my picture, she asked him who I was. He gave her my number and she had someone call me. At first I lied. I said I had a broken leg and I couldn't come in. They called me every day and I kept making up excuses. I said it would be a very long time until I could come in.

Finally, my girlfriend said she wanted to model and she was going to go in to the agency. She wanted to bring me with her for support. My hair was really short and I had on high-top purple tennis shoes, shorts, a T-shirt, and I had just finished running. I was all scrappy while she had nicely curled blond hair, and was elegantly dressed. She also brought in her portfolio of pictures. We drove to the agency together and once we got there I decided to sit and wait for her. She was in a line with all these girls who were gorgeous and beautiful. While I waited, someone came over to me and said, "You're Kristen. We know you." They remembered me from the picture the guy at work had taken. An assistant proceeded to take me in the back. I was offered a job for fifteen hundred dollars a day during Easter vacation for a German catalog in

Palm Springs. I had to step up to the plate or be completely humiliated, so I just did it.

Another time, the agent announced to me that I was booked for a commercial. When I got there, they said, "You have to sing and dance." I said, "What? What do you mean?" There were all these people looking at me. I just went nutty and did it. I was a total geek. I sang and danced, completely engaged in goofball mode. The commercial ended up winning an award. I think being forced out of my comfort zone surely raised my level of confidence.

How did you make the transition from modeling to acting?

Upon graduating from high school at the age of sixteen, my parents allowed me to move to Paris to pursue my modeling career.

I was flown over to Paris by the Elite Agency. When I got there, I had a discomforting incident with a photographer and I made the agency aware of my encounter. They instructed me that this was a large-scale client and that I should ignore the incident with the photographer. The agency failed to acknowledge my discomfort and had no regard for my dignity. Since the Elite Agency made zero effort to remedy the issue, I called the Eileen Ford affiliate of Paris. They came and got me and I made the life-changing decision to leave The Elite Agency and work for Ford. Through Ford's representation, I booked an arsenal of commercials. When I was seventeen, I moved to New York and immediately got called in to audition for the soap opera *All My Children*. There were copious amounts of girls all around the block waiting to audition. I waited in line for three hours. When I finally was able to get in and read for the show, I booked the job. I was later flown to L.A. to do a screen test with Kurt Russell for a movie called, *Tango And Cash*. I ended up booking that role as well.

A Life Changing Encounter with a Bully

Those were the two jobs that I ended up losing as the result of a temporary career paralyzing attack. I was battered and assaulted by a man as an act of gang initiation. Up until that point in my life, I always seemed to be in the right place at the right time. However, this time around that clearly wasn't the case. For his initiation the young man was required to destroy a pretty girl's face. As the selected target, my assailant succeeded in doing just that with a lead pipe. Everything in my life was derailed for quite some time. The incident left me with missing teeth, as well as several teeth that were pushed into my sinus cavity. Following the attack, I flew from New York back to L.A. to receive treatment from a team of specialists.

Given my oral and dental damage, I lost my ability to speak

normally. The gums on my right side were all gone and whatever was left was black. Currently, all the teeth on my right side are implants. It took me a few years to get back on my feet and learn to speak properly again.

Making the Best of a Bad Situation

Throughout my life, I feel like luck has always been on my side. I've been all over the world and achieved so many amazing things and had such awesome experiences. Now and then I ran into unpleasant and difficult scenarios, but they certainly don't outweigh the good. The good things that happened took some guts and required a lot of risk.

I had just gotten married before the attack, and, during the setback, my husband asked me what my biggest fears were. I had so many fears at the time that I ended up writing them all down. One of those fears was to stand as a comedian in front of an audience and get people to laugh. I said I would never do that. It would terrify me and I would crumble into a little ball. Given these self-realized fears and my inability to work at the time, my husband said, "You know what you have to do. You have to go on stage and do comedy."

I said, "Uh, no. No, no."

He followed with, "Yep. We're calling to sign you up."

Sure enough, I signed up for the comedy improv class. Every single night I went, I was terrified. I'd eat lots of candy out of nervousness, resulting in inevitable stomachaches, which would then evolve to my bowing out, saying, "I can't go."

My husband wouldn't allow it. "No, you have to go."

During the class, I was required to go on stage three times a night. Every time when I came home, I'd say, "Oh it was amazing!" I did so well that I was immediately put into the advanced class in front of a live audience. There wasn't one time that I said, "I don't remember how to do it" or "I don't know what I'm doing here." I was terrified at first, but now every time there's something I'm afraid of, or I have a knee-jerk reaction and want to say no, I tell myself, "I can do that." I still get a fair share of anxiety and consider that my career could have gone a lot better had I not been so shy.

I still have a hard time talking about myself on camera. When I've had to walk the red carpet, I'd stand there waiting and waiting, and at the last second I'd lose my nerve and run behind all the press and cameras. My agents and managers were not very happy with this nervous behavior. I'm still making focused efforts to tackle the issue of discussing myself in the spotlight. That was my goal for the past year.

I'm also saying yes to things. Somebody recently said to me, "One of our team members can't come, so we need somebody to climb to the top of the highest building with us tomorrow." I have a new part of my meditation: You have to say yes to everything today. So I said, "Oh, yes."

The next day, I found myself in L.A. climbing to the top of the highest building. I didn't know it was a race. I'm not a runner at all. I was in the middle of it and I said to myself, "Okay, just keep doing it." The expedition felt so rewarding in the end.

When you challenge yourself to do things outside your comfort zone, it's amazing how much better you feel.

I just finished filming a movie with Tom Cruise called *Jack Reacher*, and produced a film that I also star in alongside David Arquette called '*The Cottage*. Lastly, I also currently have a film out called *The Perfect Family*, starring alongside Kathleen Turner and Jason Ritter.

What would be your advice to others who are being bullied?

In some cases, experiences with bullying can plant a seed within those who are bullied. If this seed doesn't give in to the harshness of the winter and retains its roots in place, it eventually blossoms into a beautiful flower, a rose, an orchid, et cetera. Not only do those who are bullied grow stronger and more ambitious, more importantly, they can develop compassion and understanding from their own experiences. They can then help and support those who are going through the same things they have experienced. I have found that a lot of the popular people in school didn't attain any level of success or happiness later in their life. They still pine for their days of glory in high school. Interestingly, the hall monitor, science geeks, and chess club members who were picked on daily all blossomed into strong, successful, and interesting people. I think that you have to hang in there and believe that the tides will shift. It's going to change. Everybody has their time, whether it's earlier or later in life. You just have to remain strong and find things you're passionate about. Act on your interests and always keep an open mind. We each have our own place in the world. The bullies at school don't define you and they don't get to decide what kind of person you're going to be. You get to decide that.

I have a little sister who's sixteen and a nephew who's fifteen. As teenagers, they've had their fair share of issues with bullies as well. My little sister is insanely intelligent. I said to her, "Focus on school. Just be the best in school, and you'll grow to be a soaring, shining woman." She worked really hard and was chosen as one of the top five kids in her class.

During her spring break, she was sent to represent the State of California at a conference in Kenya to discuss her views on conservation and world peace. She made friends with a girl from Peru while she was there. Now she's planning to go on a student exchange in Peru for the summer. She didn't let bullies keep her down. She focused on her talents and now she's really finding her place in the world.

My nephew also had issues with bullies. In response, our family wanted to help him realize his passions. He finally discovered tennis. He didn't tell anyone in his school that he played tennis because he was sure they would ridicule him for it. Now he's becoming a champion tennis player. He's winning tournaments and entering competitions all over the country. He has such a great sense of accomplishment and his confidence is soaring.

By discovering your passion and acting on it, you will grow and gain confidence. You will also attract like-minded people on your level. Focus on your best interests, give back, be compassionate and understanding, and at the end of the day you'll realize life isn't the struggle it's made out to be. From a broader scope, bullies can serve as a catalyst to discover our potential and what we are really worth.

Section Ten

The Unwritten Letters Project

"I'm most disturbed by the theory of rubber resilience in children; as if it's much easier to bounce back with youth. I see them more like Steel. When heated, they can be bent either which way. But if it's not corrected by the time things cool down, they can be forever changed."

~Zach W. Van, author of *Inanimate Heroes*

Taking Power Away from Bullies
by Alex Boles

Alex Boles is the founder of the Unwritten Letters Project, and the author of the book, Unwritten Letters Project.

***

It's sad to say, but I honestly cannot remember a time when I wasn't being bullied. Because I've never been a skinny girl, bullying has always been a constant in my life.

The only things I remember about my childhood and teenage years are insults, bullies, doctors telling me I'm too fat, nutritionists not believing in me, and family members watching how much I eat and exercise. Instead of finding the root of a much larger genetic issue, my parents and relatives, along with the professionals I was seeing, threw every fad diet pill, exercise routine, and quick weight-loss fix at me so I could be "normal" like everyone else.

It was terrifying to wake up in the morning with the fear that someone might ask me how much I weighed. What's even worse is the fact that I cannot remember a time when I did not feel this way. So at the ages of ten, thirteen, sixteen, twenty, and even today, I walk through my house, grocery stores, theaters, and doctor's offices still sucking it all in. I'm constantly glancing behind and around me to see if someone is watching me or making a disgusted face at the fact that I'm not like everyone else. I'm not like them. I grew up as an outcast.

Even though I was very involved in school and actually had a lot of friends, I was severely bullied in every level of my education. Making myself more visible in the school by being involved in student council, theater, and other clubs made me more of a target. I always stood out because of my body weight. I had to be true to myself, and blending in and trying to play it safe never worked for me. When I was successful, there were always more people trying to tear me down.

Middle school is a time when kids are self-conscious and trying to fit in. My peers seemed to feel that they could build themselves up by tearing other people down. I had a difficult time with numerous bullies, but there's one specific girl who really stands out. She'd torment me in classes, scream insults through the hallways between classes, giggle and make fun of me when I walked by. She managed to make me hate school and everything it represented.

I joined the student mediation club, where I helped my peers navigate through their issues with each other. When my bullying issue became so bad that it was affecting everything that mattered to me as a twelve-year-old, I tried to seek help through the school counselor. The school's solution to bullying was to bring the bully in for a mediation session with the counselor. Although this showed the bully that her behavior was being watched, it didn't solve the problem. The only time my parents remember me talking to them about being bullied was when things became so bad with this girl that I came home hysterical and demanded that I be transferred to a different school. My parents seriously contemplated homeschooling, but I actually just went back to school.

Bullying has been a factor in molding my personality over the years. I enter every relationship, whether friendly or romantic, with a constant fear of judgment and criticism. I'm always waiting for judgments about what I'm eating, why I'm eating, or to be told I need to work out. Because of these feelings, I don't ever let people get close to me. My insecurities affect who I trust—and every aspect of my life, really.

My mom always asks me why I don't date. She even tells people I don't like dating. Honestly, after being bullied my entire life because of the way I look, it's really hard to enter into a game where the first judgment is always based on appearance. People who haven't had to deal with that just don't understand. Why would I voluntarily put myself into a situation to be criticized? I'm holding out and not taking opportunities that could change my life because I'm scared of judgment. So that's how bullying has really changed me.

Discovering the Problem

I became really sick during my sophomore year of college. I went to seven doctors and had to have a lymph node biopsy to find out I had mono. In the process of this illness, one doctor actually took the time to figure out why I didn't look like my other three sisters. He never asked me how much I ate, and he never told me I was overweight. Instead, he told me he would actually try to figure out why I was overweight instead of trying to "fix" me with fad remedies that never work.

It turned out that I have polycystic ovarian syndrome. This condition could have been recognized when I was ten years old, but, instead, doctors focused on the fat, not the person. Polycystic ovarian syndrome is a lack of insulin in the ovaries, creating an insulin deficiency, estrogen deficiency, and metabolism decrease, among other symptoms. It treats the body a lot like diabetes and I need to take Metformin, a drug administered to diabetics, to regulate the syndrome in my body.

My doctor basically told me that until a doctor diagnosed me with this syndrome and put me on Metformin, I was "fighting a losing battle" with my weight. Diet pills won't work, exercising won't work, bullying me for eating *won't work!* A simple blood test could have given me the answer.

I wouldn't have wasted thirteen years trying to figure out why I could work out every day, be a vegetarian for a year, and eat the same amount as a one hundred-pound girl and still weigh twice as much. I wouldn't have to deal with all the issues I'm dealing with because of the bullies in my life. But I'm who I am today because of my bullies, and I know that there is a reason, some reason, that I didn't find this information out until my mid-twenties.

My mom asked me once, "Would you be the person you are today, helping people, if you would have grown up thin?" As much as I would like to say, "Of course, Mom," the truth is, I honestly don't know, but I don't have to know because I didn't grow up thin. I grew up me, and so I decided to try to help those like me, and that's what I'm still doing today.

The Unwritten Letters Project
by Alex Boles

The April following my diagnosis, I started a website called the "Unwritten Letters Project."

Mission Statement: The Unwritten Letters Project is created to empower others by providing a safe, judgment-free outlet that encourages participants to articulate, heal from, and overcome hardships.

I kept a journal pretty religiously growing up, detailing the boys who hassled me, the girls who laughed at me, and the feelings that poured out of me at night. Sometimes I would write letters to people I knew I'd never stand up to. Sometimes I'd write letters to people I wanted to be friends with but I knew they wouldn't accept me because I was overweight. I took this format and made it into a platform for everyone around the world to use.

But having a successful, interactive website wasn't my goal when I was starting out. My goal has always been to make a difference in people who are dealing with bullies, whether these bullies are actual people or your own thoughts which you use against yourself. I want people to stand up to the bullies, realize they have a voice, and get that voice out in writing when it's hard to say the words out loud. Of course, the site has turned into much more than just facing your internal or external demons. People write letters to anyone, alive or deceased. It gives them a way to share the feelings they might never have had the opportunity to share while the offender was still alive.

The Unwritten Letters Project has received a decent amount of online attention, thanks in large part to social media and my university, so I decided to self-publish a volume of letters in the fall of 2009.

When I realized that I can make an impact on people globally, I decided to start a Bullying and Suicide Prevention Campaign through the Unwritten Letters Project. I began to partner with national and local organizations and gear readers toward participating in other efforts around the world as well.

Because the issue of bullying is so personal for me, I know now that this is probably one of the reasons why I didn't find out about the polycystic ovarian syndrome until my twenties. Sometimes the people who have been through the worst of situations are the ones who can guide others with similar problems out of unhealthy situations and into a better life. I never personally went through depression or had any thoughts of suicide, but bullying is one of the major contributing factors in teen suicides. If writing a letter, reading the letters of others, reading my personal story, or getting information about bullying and suicide prevention on my site saves one life, then it was all worth it.

The energy and passion for helping people that I took from every person who bullied me is saving lives every day. In my mind, I see myself taking a little bit of power away from my bullies every time I post a new letter. And every time I get a letter addressed to me or the Unwritten Letters Project detailing how I've helped someone get through their self-harm or depression, I know I am making a difference.

Bullying changed me for sure. I still secretly wish I grew up "normal." But there are ways to come out a better person after bullying. It does get better. I have the courage to tell my story and stand up to the people who bullied me because when you stand united, you can make a difference in those who are still faltering on their knees. Find the rainbow through the rain because once the sky clears, it really is a beautiful day.

Letters to Bullies
by various authors

Dear Bully,

I now know that everyone's put into my life for a reason or a learning lesson. Of course, at eight years old, I didn't know what the reason was. I already had abuse at home, so your bullying just added to my pot of water that was coming to a boil. Every day after school, I dreaded getting on my bus to go home and get off at the same bus stop as you did. It hurt to see you happy to hide behind a tree, waiting for me to get off the bus so you could beat me up. It was worse during the winter when it was freezing outside to be thrown into the snow and kicked in the face and ribs by you. The snow actually helped to numb the pain. I didn't feel a thing. My mother didn't believe me when I told her that you were bullying me. I received no support or help.

I believe it was my angel or guide who helped me to stand up and not take any more from you. I remember this day crystal clear. My last period bell rang, and I gathered every single book and object in my locker. My bag was so heavy, I could barely carry it. I got on that bus and when it came to our stop, you had barely come out from behind the tree. I took my heavy book bag and knocked you out. When you came to, you were crying and ran away like a coward. I can't say I felt bad at the time. I didn't have an ounce of remorse. I felt good that you didn't get to beat me up that time.

That night, your mother called my mother, and my mother dragged me to the hospital to apologize to you. I looked straight into your mother's eyes and said, "I'm not apologizing to your monster son; he has been beating me up every day after school for months!" Your mother was horrified to think that her son was such a bully, and you admitted it to everyone. I thank you for that. I was sorry for putting you in the hospital, but, obviously, that's what it took for you to finally stop bullying me.

Ever since then, you were the nicest guy in school; you really turned out to be a nice guy. I thank you for those changes. I understood you had problems at home, too. I'm just glad you turned yourself around and turned out to be such a great guy. You apologized to me years later, too, and I appreciate that. I see you are married with kids now and I can sincerely wish you happiness.

~Chinhee Park

***

Dear Bully,

You tried to harm my sister and put her in a dark and helpless place just because she wanted to go to a gay club and listen to music. You went off on her verbally about how disrespectful it was to you and proceeded to physically assault her. She was able to get away from you, but she was out of state and left you in a hurry with no money. Sunhee called me up and asked if I could send her money, but I was also broke. My sister went to the ATM and there was three hundred dollars in the account. She thought I put the money in there, but I didn't. To this day, we have no idea where the money came from. Sunhee then went to the airport and spoke to a rep. The woman saw my sister had been brutally beaten and checked for airfares back to N.Y. The ticket was around five hundred dollars because it was last minute. The manager came out and saw my sister and immediately told her that they would only charge her a hundred dollars, since she only had three hundred dollars. That way, she could have some money for other things. My sister was in tears because of the total strangers who showed her love and compassion. This is not what was shown to her by you, the man who should have loved her, but instead beat her and left her alone in a strange city.

When she came home to New York, that night she felt major energy going through her hands. She focused this healing energy on her injuries. Her severe bruises and cuts were almost gone the next day. Sunhee had healed herself. I was stunned and amazed. The negative bullying energy you used to assault my sister caused her to realize the gifts that were inside her. This was the day she became aware of her physical healing abilities.

The other bullies in our lives used verbal insults. They made fun of us because we were Korean, imitating the Korean language—that we didn't even speak!—in a mocking way, and stretching their eyes with their fingers to make their eyes slanted. I never felt so ugly before in my life. I wanted to get surgery on my eyes to make them look like other American kids'. It caused us to feel so insecure and hate the fact we were Korean.

The first time I heard the comment from my girlfriend, "You have the most beautiful eyes," I didn't believe her. After that, I kept hearing from friends and strangers that they loved my eyes. We were told that our eyes are so beautiful they could look at them all day. Thanks to them, we started to love our eyes, and I no longer wanted surgery. What we've learned from these bullies is that they were put in our lives to show us the obvious difference between love and hate. When I started to hate myself, it was such a dark place to be. The moment I started to love myself, I felt love around me and the darkness vanished. Being a psychic healer and empathic, I learned from a spiritual aspect that we, as sensitive people, pick up empathy from other people's thoughts, emotions, and feelings. I didn't really hate myself; I was picking up empathy from the bully's hate for himself. I was able to put myself in his shoes and instead of hating him, have compassion for him. That was the best way to heal from everything and to still have love and compassion for people who weren't capable of loving us. We are sending tons of love to all the victims, and I encourage you to try to find the *good* out of anything *bad*!

Love,
Chinhee & Sunhee Park

***

Letter to Those I've Bullied

I look back at how mean I was to some people and just want to cry! I'm so sorry that I tortured them the way I did. Maybe, since I was hurting, I wanted others to hurt?

My oldest son is a people pleaser, and a great kid! He likes to go with the flow and not ruffle anyone's feathers. When he was in fourth grade, there was a kid in his class who was a bully to others. He even bullied my son, although my son said he would just ignore it. I told my son then and I tell my fifth grader now how to deal with bullies.

The best defense to handling bullies is to act indifferent and just ignore it. Walk away and don't respond.

I know this is hard, but after a few times of this, the bully should lose interest. Bullies want a reaction from you. You may also try using humor.

For example: If a bully says, "Nice shoes. Where'd you get them—from the trash?"

Response: "How'd you know? Were they your shoes?" Or, "Yeah, I'm all about recycling!" Or you can return with a question: "Why do you care what shoes I wear?"

I've found the best method is the indifferent response, as it is neither engaging nor antagonizing.

I'm now very sensitive about defending kids any time I see bullying going on, and stress to my two boys that it is *never* okay.

I wish I could go back in time and change how I treated others, but I can't. So I'll say now, I'm so very sorry for any hurt that I caused you. It was a *terrible* thing to do. You didn't deserve it. Please forgive me for my actions!

Thank you.

~Jacki from Wisconsin

Letter to the Bullies

You'll probably never know the effect you had on me when I was at school. Never know the dread I'd feel wondering if today would be like every other day or if today the bullying would stop. You probably never knew what it felt like to want to fit in and not be the butt of every joke, and I hope you never will. Many of you are mothers now and I hope your children never have to face what I did because of your words and actions. I hope you realize that what you said and did was wrong, that picking on an innocent person didn't make you feel any better. Being a bully didn't make you a smarter, prettier, or better person. I hope that if you see someone else being bullied today, you've learned to help them rather than joining in. It only takes one person to make a difference.

from
Rachel

***

To My Bullies:

I want you to know that the things you said and did to me will affect me for life in ways I don't even know about yet. You tried to make me give up on my dreams by making me feel worthless. But I want you to know that instead, I used that feeling to drive me to go after my dreams even harder! And now, every day my dreams are coming true!

Beyond this, I want you to know that I truly feel sorry for you. I'm sorry for whatever happened in your life that made you feel like you needed to bully me. I'm sorry for whoever made you feel worthless, and I'm sorry that you didn't learn to treat others how you wanted to be treated. I hope that one day, you get to the point in life where you can become happy enough inside where you don't feel the need to bully others in an attempt to make yourself feel better.

Fierce & Love,
Daniel Joseph Baker

***

Dear Miss Bully,

I know you're picking on me at work and making up policies that only seem to apply to me. I know you talk about me behind my back, and I know you showed my co-worker my salary—that's why she's wondering why I make more than others. I also know you're trying to set me up and place a cap on my salary for the next review. I know you looked at my resume and asked me for my experience because you're trying to intimidate me. But what you don't know is that I don't intimidate easily.

You pick on me because you're insecure, and you know that when you blink too long, they'll offer me your job. You pick on me because you have less experience than I do and you're trying to dominate me and ensure that I know you're the supervisor. You don't supervise me, and that makes you angry. I make just as much salary as you do, and maybe more. I have twice as much education as you, and you fear. I know the color of my skin makes it even more upsetting for you.

I want you to know that I love the fact that you fear losing your job to me, and that I make you feel insecure. But know this—each time you pick on me, I am also building a case against you and HR already knows, so by the end of this year or maybe next year, your insecurities will soon be confirmed. Hate on me some more for the color of my skin—it will only speed up the process.

Thanks.
Keesha Parsons,
CEO Mesonista.com - Fashion Style Guide
Email: parsons@mesonista.com

***

Dear Bullies,

In so many ways, I want to scream at the top of my lungs and tell you how much you ruined my life growing up. I want to ask you why you had to be so mean just because I was overweight. I want to cry and tell you that you made me hate myself every day. You made me think no one would think I was ever good enough. I want to tell you that I deserve to be happy in a relationship, but I am terrified of telling any man how I feel for fear of rejection and criticism. I hate that I gave you power and still give you power by letting you control my confidence in many situations.

I wish I could go back to middle school and stand up to you and tell you that you're only being mean because you're so insecure with yourself that you need to demean people to be some pathetic form of "happy." I want to tell every boy who laughed at the thought of me liking him that a woman is not defined by her body weight, but by her mind. A woman at two hundred pounds deserves love and happiness just as much as a woman at a hundred and twenty pounds.

Part of me wants to punish you for every ounce of pain you made me feel, but I know that's not the way to handle this situation. One day, you'll look back at your life and realize you were a bully. Maybe you'll feel remorse. Maybe you won't. But if I don't become a better person, then I've let you win. So, bully, instead of staying in the small place where you left me in middle school, I've decided to create a much bigger space and let anyone join me in creating positive energy. I don't want to thank you for how you treated me, but I'll let you know that I've realized that I'm better than the bullies in my life. I can overcome your negativity and share what I've learned with those who're still hiding in the small places where they're being held hostage by bullies. I don't know why you picked on me. I don't know why you thought it was okay to make people hate themselves, but hopefully one day, you'll realize that even you're not perfect. Maybe you should've been nicer to the kid in middle school who would've accepted you with all your imperfections. So why couldn't you accept me for all my imperfections, too?

> Better because of you,
> Alexandria Boles

***

Dear Bully,

I hope your life turned out better than it seemed destined to when last we met. I hope you made peace with whatever demons that drove you to torment me. Perhaps you have found counseling; if not, I hope you do. You may have given me a few setbacks, but I learned to fly and now am doing all I can to make the world a better place, getting accolades, community service awards, and writing awards for the work I do. I hope you are doing as much to make amends for your past, but more importantly, to make a future in which no one feels the need to belittle others to feel better about themselves. A world in which diversity is celebrated and all people are treated with respect. That is what I'm trying to do. I hope you will join me in this effort.

> ~Matt Ivester

***

Dear Bully,

I was reminiscing about a time back in high school when I felt that you and a couple of the teammates were always picking on and bullying me. I never spoke out about this until recently, when I was asked to contribute to an article on bullying. The way I was treated bothered me to no end. Many days I was scared to even come to basketball practice because of the painful experiences you and your friends would put me through.

I was fortunate to have a network of coaches, teachers, and mentors who helped me develop from the shy, insecure, uncoordinated kid you'd see in the locker room during our sophomore and junior years in high school. With their support, I've developed into the man I am today. I hold no grudges or hate toward you, only a sense of sympathy because I now realize how lonely and frustrating life can be for the typical bully.

We happened to bump into each other recently during a visit to our hometown, and I appreciated you coming up to me and reintroducing yourself. The years have *flown* by, and we're all starting to show our wear and tear and carry with us the lines and wrinkles of experience. I was happy for our brief chat, and I want you to know that I carry no ill will toward you. I know that you're a little embarrassed about some of the experiences that you've gone through recently (unemployment, near homelessness, divorce, substance abuse) before finding God, etc., but I do wish you well.

Perhaps the experience of being bullied by you and some of your friends prepared me for life's challenges that are sure to fall upon all of us. I'm just glad that I was able to find the proper channels and support to help me along the way. I pray the same for you.

~James Donaldson

***

Randy,

I started roller skating when I was about seven years old. By the time I was thirteen, I was competing in speed skating. I considered the roller rink as my territory. It was the place where I felt safe. One day when I was thirteen, you came into the rink with a couple of your cronies and started making fun of me. It really made me mad that you had the nerve to invade my territory. I skated by you, and you reached out and shoved me down. I got so mad that instead of punching you, I skated up to you and swung my arm out straight with the palm of my hand. I hit you so hard that it pulled my arm back and broke my wrist, but I hit you so hard I knocked you out. I was in pain, but I said to the other guys, "Okay, which one of you is next?" I knew if one of them stepped forward, I would be in trouble because I was hurting so bad it made me sick. Neither one of them wanted to fight me once they saw me knock you out.

I'm strong now. I am a black belt in karate and I have a wife and family. Bullies like you tried to keep me down, but never succeeded.

~Markus Horner

Dear Bully,

You're only using your rage and intimidation because of your own fear. I know you're afraid. All you really want is acceptance and maybe your mom or dad doesn't give it to you, or maybe they're dead and gone, divorced, or in jail, and maybe you were hurt. Because you were hurt, you stood up and now you're mean to people. But really, you're not mean. You just don't want to be hurt. It's easier to be the one who hurts others rather than being hurt yourself. Don't do it. You're a beautiful human being. Holy sh**! I mean, seriously!!! You are matter and particles and atoms that are freakin' standing and talking and dancing! Like, how could you *not* see how amazing you are? Be strong! Don't let this #$%# world beat you down to the point where you think you need to be mean or violent. Be strong. Be brave enough to love yourself and others.

John Wright
Model, actor, Hollywood producer

***

Dear Bully,

I wanted to let you know you robbed me of my freshman year high school experience.

Your acts of terror were constant, and you never let up on the barrage of insults and jokes at my expense. Now I have a great sense of humor.

You would push me, throw things at me, and even threaten to "pay me a visit" at my house. Now I know several forms of martial arts.

You told my friends not to hang out with me because I was gay and would give them diseases. Now I have more friends and acquaintances than ever before in my life.

You made me afraid to go to school, afraid to get out of bed when so many kids were excited to see new friends and have new experiences. I wrote my first book about it at age eighteen.

Everything you did to me to ruin me... made me better in some way. I'm just curious to know, what did it do for you?

Sincerely,
The "Victim"
Zack W. Van

P.S. You robbed me of my freshman year of high school, but not much else.

Centered: ***

Dear Bully,
You have made me think less of myself for your own pleasure. I realize now that no one is perfect. I should never have let you get inside me like you did. No one should judge another person for how they decide to live their life. It doesn't matter how old you are, you will always find a pointless reason to hate me, and you won't be happy until I'm unhappy. I'm here to tell you now that I'm not afraid, nor am I concerned about what you say or think of me. You aren't a queen and you aren't in charge of my life. You are a human no better than me. Jealousy is such an ugly thing. It can turn the nicest person into a horrible monster on the inside. You felt pleasure in making me feel weak and powerless.

This is not a hate note, but a thank you. Yes, thank you for showing me that my life was so important to you that you were always focused on what I was doing. I find it comforting that you worry so much about what I'm doing. This letter is the last thought I have of you. All the hurtful things you've said are absolutely pointless now. I promise you that you're wasting your time on me. I will live my life to the fullest. Your hate, jealousy, and actions will never slow me down or cross my mind. I forgive you. You have made me stronger and better prepared to face ignorant people like yourself.

Everyone has a voice and should use it against people like you. My foot has been permanently down and will stand against bullies and the hurtful things they say. I am a talented young woman with goals and standards. Will I let you get in the way of my happiness? No, never again. And that's a promise.

Savanna Peterson
Age 18
Co-Author of *Drugs Make You Un-Smarter*

Centered: ***

Dear Bully,
You really suck! Everything you have done to me and continue to do to others, to this very day, hurts. But now that I have moved houses, communities, and schools I'm sort of happy you've bullied me because I've learned not to share secrets and not to trust people so easily.

Even though I was bullied for the past two years of school, it feels like it was long ago because I have so many new friends. I'm starting to forget about how you've made me feel.

202

Now that I'm writing this letter, I realize that what you've done to me can no longer control me. I'm sure that now you have a new victim and have forgotten all about me.

I wish you'd just stop!

Sincerely,
Abby
Age 13

List of Resources

Organizations and Websites:
Are you a victim of a crime? National Center for Victims of Crime: http://www.ncvc.org or Office of Victims of Crime http://www.ovc.org

Are you gay or think you might be gay? Gay Lesbian and Straight Education Network: http://www.glsen.org

Ask the Judge: Answers for teens about the law: http://www.askthejudge.info/

Breaking Down Barriers: The Chris Hendrick Band speaks to youth about bullying: http://www.chrishendricksmusic.com/

Bullies to Buddies, the simple solution to bullying http://bullies2buddies.com/

By Parents-forParents.com

Dealing with Bullying: Kid Health.org, http://kidshealth.org/teen/your_mind/problems/bullies.html

Human Rights Campaign: http://www.hrc.org

Kid Power: http://www.kidpower.org/bullying/

No Bully Beat.org. Drumming away barriers and bullying: http://drumbus.com/no-bully-beat-information-flyer/

Pacers National Bullying Prevention Center: http://www.pacer.org/bullying/

Stomp out Bullying: http://www.stompoutbullying.org/

Stop Bullying.gov. What is bullying, Cyberbullying, who's at risk? Prevent bullying: http://www.stopbullying.gov/

Stop Bullying Now organization: http://www.stopbullyingnowfoundation.org/main/

Suicide Hotline 1-800-Suicide 1-800-784-2433 or 1-800-273-Talk 1-800-273-8255

The Human Rights Education Center of Utah: http://hrecutah.org/

Thirty Best Colleges for LGBT Students: http://www.bestcolleges.com/features/best-colleges-for-lgbt

Violence Prevention Works, the world foremost bullying prevention program: http://www.violencepreventionworks.org/public/index.page

Books:

Aiden's Waltz byVictoria Marin, about rising above autism. www.aidenswaltz.com

Bullies to Buddies, How to Turn Your Enemies into Friends by Izzie Kalman

Bullying—What Adults Need to Know to Keep Kids Safe by Irene Van der Zande

Consistently Persistent: Living with Tourette's Trifecta by Mark Horner http://www.amazon.com/Consistently-Persistent-Living-Tourette-Trifecta

How to Save Our Children from Crime, Drugs and Violence by Cedric Dean

Inanimate Heroes by Zack Van Den Berge, about a boy who was bullied because he was gay.

KidPower Book for Caring Adults by Irene van der Zande

lol … OMG! What Every Student Needs to Know About Online Reputation Management, Digital Citizenship and Cyberbullying by Matt Ivester

Peace2U: Three-Phase Bullying Solution and *Peace Be With You: Christ-Centered Bullying Solution, curricula for teacher and counselors* http://ace.nd.edu/press/ by Frank DiLallo Published by ACE Press at the University of Notre Dame

Rounding Third by Walter G. Meyer. This book deals quite powerfully with teens being bullied until one of them can't take it anymore and attempts suicide.

Teen Cyberbullying Investigated: Where Do Your Rights End and Consequences Begin by Tom Jacobs. This book is endorsed by Dr. Phil McGraw.

The Heart of Applebutter Hill—about being legally blind by Donna Hill--http://donnawhill.com/ (Sales of this book help blind students)

The Respectful School: How Educators and Students can Conquer Hate and Harassment by Stephen Wessler and William Preble

Transcending Fear: The Journey to Freedom and Fulfillment by Victoria Reynolds www.victoriamreynolds.com

Transforming School Climate and Learning: Beyond Bullying and Compliance by William Preble and Rick M. Gordon

About the Author

Jill Ammon Vanderwood is a mother and grandmother from Salt Lake City, Utah. She experienced bullying while she was in the fifth grade. One boy even brought a gas mask to school for his friend who sat next to her in class.

Jill is the published author of six other books, including the Mom's Choice Award winning book, *Drugs Make You Un-Smarter*, coauthored by her teenage granddaughter, Savanna Peterson and *What's It Like, Living Green? Kids Teaching Kids, by the Way They Live.*

Jill is an experienced speaker and is available to speak at your conference, school, youth group, or camp.

You can find Jill on the Web at www.jillvanderwood.com

ALL THINGS THAT MATTER PRESS

FOR MORE INFORMATION ON TITLES AVAILABLE FROM
ALL THINGS THAT MATTER PRESS, GO TO
http://allthingsthatmatterpress.com
or contact us at
allthingsthatmatterpress@gmail.com

www.ingramcontent.com/pod-product-compliance
Lightning Source LLC
Chambersburg PA
CBHW071426090426
42737CB00011B/1582